LAWPACK™

DO-IT-YOURSELF

Separation
& Divorce

Separation & Divorce
by Maureen Mullally

Published by
Lawpack Publishing Limited
76-89 Alscot Road
London SE1 3AW

www.lawpack.co.uk

First edition 2003
Reprinted 2004

ISBN: 1 904053 32 7

Printed in Great Britain

Important facts

This Lawpack Guide contains the information, instruction and completed examples of forms necessary to handle your own divorce without a solicitor.

This Guide is for people seeking a divorce in England or Wales. It is not suitable for use in Scotland or Northern Ireland. The law is stated as at 1 July 2004.

The information it contains has been carefully compiled from professional sources, but its accuracy is not guaranteed, as laws and regulations may change or be subject to differing interpretations.

Neither this nor any other publication can take the place of a solicitor on important legal matters. As with any legal matter, common sense should determine whether you need the assistance of a solicitor rather than relying solely on the information and forms in this Lawpack Guide.

We strongly urge you to consult a solicitor if:

- substantial amounts of money are involved;

- you do not understand the instructions or are uncertain as to how to complete and use a form correctly;

- what you want to do is not precisely covered by the forms provided.

About the author

Maureen Mullally studied law at King's College, University of London. Afterwards, she was called to the Bar at Gray's Inn in London and also to the Irish Bar at King's Inns in Dublin.

She has practised as a barrister specialising in family law for over 25 years and now works as a mediator in family disputes.

Maureen writes a weekly column on family and legal matters in the *Universe* newspaper. She has been interviewed on family law matters on *Woman's Hour*, *The Jimmy Young Show* and other radio programmes and has contributed feature articles to *YOU Magazine*, *Good Housekeeping*, *The Times*, the *Daily Mail*, the *Family Law Journal* and *Woman's Realm*.

She is a member of the Southwark Diocesan Child Protection Commission and a Board Member of the Catholic Children's Society.

Her previous publications include *Law and the Family* and *Law and the Family in Ireland* (Blackhall).

Maureen would like to thank Karen Graham, of Macdonald Graham, Solicitors, Bath, for her help in reviewing the text.

Table of contents

How to use this book ....*vii*

Introduction ....*viii*

Overview ....*ix*

1   Thinking about divorce 1

2   Judicial separation and deeds of separation 7

3   Can you handle your own divorce? 11

4   The grounds for divorce...............................17

5   Mediation 21

6   Protecting yourself during divorce.......................23

7   Who gets what when you split up?...........................27

8   Children and the law 41

9   Caring for the children 45

10   Children – reports to the court 57

11   Child support...65

12   Child abuse...71

13   Domestic violence.......................................79

14   Child abduction.......................................87

15   Eight steps to divorce 97

Glossary of useful terms *109*

Appendix...*113*

Index..*201*

How to use this book

This Lawpack Guide can help you achieve an important legal objective conveniently, efficiently and economically. Remember that it is important for you to use this Guide properly if you are to avoid later difficulties.

Step-by-step instructions for using this Guide

1. Read this Guide carefully. If after thorough examination you decide that your requirements are not met by this Lawpack Guide, or you do not feel confident about writing your own documents, consult a solicitor.

2. At the end of this Guide there are completed examples of the forms needed to handle your own divorce. Contact your local County court, listed in the telephone directory, to obtain copies of these forms.

3. Once obtained, make several copies of the original forms for practice, for future use and for updates. You should also make copies of the completed forms. Create a record-keeping system for both sets of copies.

4. When completing a form, do not leave any section blank. If any section is inapplicable, write 'not applicable' or 'none'. This shows you have not overlooked the section.

5. Always use pen or type on legal documents; never use pencil.

6. Do not cross out or erase anything you have written on your final forms.

7. You will find a helpful glossary of terms at the end of this Lawpack Guide. Refer to this glossary if you find unfamiliar terms.

8. Always keep legal documents in a safe place and in a location known to your spouse, family, executor or solicitor.

Introduction

The end of a marriage can be a messy, expensive and traumatic time, or it can be a sad but necessary stage on the path to new lives for you, your spouse and your children.

This Lawpack Guide aims to help you help yourself. By being aware in advance of the problems you may encounter and the issues that need resolution, you can prepare to deal with them in an atmosphere of negotiated agreement rather than arbitrary and hurtful dispute. This Guide should also save you money at a time when financial concerns may well be troubling you.

If you and your spouse agree that divorce is necessary, the procedure can be quite straightforward; it is often possible to avoid using a solicitor at this stage. Issues concerning the distribution of the property you both own and questions of contact with children and where they will live can also be resolved by agreement, although property issues need to be endorsed by the court.

However, this Lawpack Guide is not a substitute for professional legal advice. If you are at all unsure of your rights or what you can reasonably expect from divorce, you should seek professional advice (see Appendix).

An overview guide to a simple undefended divorce

1

Petitioner sends to court

Petition and three copies (*Form D8*)

Statement of Arrangements for Children and two copies (*Form D8A*)

Original Marriage Certificate

Fee or application for exemption

2

Respondent receives from court

Copy of Petition (*Form D8*)

Statement of Arrangements for Children for signature (*Form D8A*)

Notice of Proceedings

Acknowledgment of Service

3

Respondent sends to petitioner

Acknowledgment of Service with consent to divorce

4

Court sends to petitioner

Notice of Issue of Petition

5

Petitioner sends to court

Application for Directions for Trial (*Form D84*)

Affidavit of Evidence (*Form D80*)

6

District judge

Considers arrangements for children and divorce papers

Issues certificate of entitlement to decree

7

Court pronounces decree nisi

Provisional divorce pending resolution of financial and
other matters. Attendance not usually required

8

(After six weeks)

Petitioner sends to court

Application for Decree Nisi to be made Absolute (*Form D36*)

Court sends decree absolute

Now the divorce is complete

Chapter 1:
Thinking about divorce

A history

In 1936, King Edward VIII, having succeeded to the throne, found himself in an extremely difficult position. He had fallen deeply in love with Wallis Simpson. Wallis was an American and, to make matters worse, she was a divorcée. The King desperately wanted to marry her and, at the same time, keep the throne, but it was made clear to him by his advisers that this was impossible. Even though he was hugely popular with the people, at that time it was simply unthinkable for him to marry a divorcée. He made his choice and abdicated in favour of his brother, the father of Queen Elizabeth II. Edward VIII became the Duke of Windsor, married Wallis, and lived in exile from Britain for the rest of his life. Sometimes it seems hard to believe that all this happened less than 70 years ago.

In the early 1950s, Princess Margaret, sister of Queen Elizabeth, fell in love with Group Captain Peter Townsend. Peter was in many ways a suitable match for a princess, having had a distinguished wartime service career, followed by a stint serving as one of Buckingham Palace's most trusted courtiers. But he too had been divorced. Like her uncle before her, Princess Margaret was faced with a stark choice. She chose her duty, and she and the Group Captain had to part.

When you contrast these two pieces of history with the present day, you realise how our attitudes to divorce have changed over a few short decades. Princess Margaret herself was divorced from her husband in 1978 and three out of the Queen's four children have been through the heartbreak and trauma of marital breakdown. Sadly none of this is very unusual as the rate of divorce has increased to almost fifty per cent of all marriages celebrated today.

However, people still do not appear to be discouraged by this harsh statistic. In more than a third of today's marriages the husband, the wife or both partners are having another shot at marital bliss. Some husbands and wives are attempting it for the third, fourth or even fifth time!

It is difficult to say why so many marriages are breaking down today. Years ago, when most people were committed to a religion and attended church regularly, marriage was bolstered by faith. Marriage was a sacrament, an undertaking until death intervened. Only the church had any power over marriage; divorce was a possibility but quite rare.

No doubt some marriages were unhappy, but most people had very little expectation of married happiness. Marriages were usually arranged between the families of the bride and groom with the young people themselves having very little say in the arrangements, particularly if any property was involved. However, remarriage was fairly common because people generally had a much shorter life span. Many mothers did not survive childbirth and most diseases were incurable due to medicine being in its infancy. As a result, a husband or wife lucky enough to enjoy good health might have outlived several spouses and remarried several times.

Once the civil courts took over from the church in deciding upon divorce, a husband and a wife did not come to the court on equal terms. The husband would usually ask for a divorce as he was the one with the money. In those rare cases where a wife attempted to divorce her husband, she was still disadvantaged. A husband could get a divorce simply on the ground that his wife had committed adultery but if a wife wanted to divorce her husband on the same ground, she had to prove that the adultery had been incestuous or had been coupled with bigamy, rape, sodomy, bestiality or cruelty.

A woman with children who was found to have committed adultery could lose her children forever, no matter how young they were. In contrast, an adulterous father would not have had to suffer such a separation. Children then belonged to their fathers, who could do pretty much as they pleased with them.

In circumstances where you had committed adultery and were asking for a divorce yourself, you might be refused the divorce. If you were a divorced person you were someone to be shunned, particularly if you happened to be a woman. A person who had a decree of divorce pronounced against him or her would be particularly stigmatised as being the 'guilty' party.

Irretrievable breakdown

In 1969, an attempt was made to abolish the idea that there had to be a guilty party in every divorce case. It was decided that the only ground for divorce should be the irretrievable breakdown of the marriage – in other words that there could only be a divorce in cases where there was no hope whatsoever of the marriage surviving.

Unfortunately, Parliament then went on to decide that the breakdown had to be demonstrated in one of five ways. These were: (i) adultery; (ii) unreasonable behaviour; (iii) desertion for two years; (iv) living apart for two years if both partners agreed to a divorce; (v) living apart for five years, even if one of the partners did not want a divorce.

To be accused of committing adultery, or of behaving so unreasonably that your husband or wife should not be expected to live with you have, not surprisingly, continued to inflame emotions. Going through a divorce is still one of the most stressful experiences that anyone can have, and being branded as the guilty party just makes matters worse. The truth is that in the majority of divorces there is no guilty party and no innocent party. Marriages break down for all sorts of reasons, but it generally takes two to break a marriage just as it takes two to make one successful.

Help with problems

No one should ever rush into a divorce. It is important to consider whether there is any possibility that expert counselling might be able to help. Over time, problems may work themselves out. Anger dissolves; feelings change. With patience, you and your spouse may be able to resolve your difficulties. No matter how black things may look to you, it may well be that there is a way to save your relationship.

The first thing to realise is that the marriage in which there have never been any problems is something that does not exist. It is not an admission of failure if you are having difficulties. But if things are going wrong you are likely to feel confused, unhappy and uncertain about what is the right thing to do.

For those who need clarity, Relate, which used to be called the Marriage Guidance Council, provides the principal counselling service for people having relationship problems. Relate has centres all over the country and over half a century of experience of helping couples in trouble. It offers counselling to couples whether they are married or unmarried.

Relate counsellors are carefully selected and trained. Their training teaches them what makes relationships work – and what works against good relationships. They do not adopt a superior attitude. They do not 'tell people off', act as judges or preach. Unshockable, they are trained above all to listen, and what they hear is treated with the strictest confidence.

The atmosphere at Relate centres is as relaxed and friendly as possible, with paper hankies always at the ready. The problems people bring to the counsellors are as varied as the people themselves – inability to talk to a partner or to persuade a partner to talk to them, loneliness, jealousy and problems with children or in-laws are common examples.

Relate emphasise that the time to come for counselling, if possible, is when the problems first arise. Waiting for them to resolve themselves may mean that by the time counselling is sought it is too late because things have already got themselves into such a mess. However, that does not mean that counselling can never help when problems have existed for a long time. Couples can be helped at any stage.

Your local telephone directory should have the number of your local Relate centre, where you can make an appointment for an initial interview. At that interview the counsellor will discuss the best kind of help for you. It might be that one, two or three sessions will be necessary to help. You might need more.

Obviously, if both you and your partner go together, counselling is likely to be more successful but even if your partner refuses to go, counselling can often help. If things do begin to improve between you as a result of the counselling sessions, your partner might be persuaded to come with you.

What the counsellor does during the sessions is to try to help you to understand your relationship, the problems which have come up, the possible causes of them, and the various choices available to you as solutions. The counsellor then helps you to work out your own answers to the problems. He or she does not tell you what to do. It is for you to consider the options open to you and to choose the one that seems best.

Counsellors will not try to persuade you to stay together. They know how damaging a divorce can be, especially when there are children in the family, but they are realistic. They recognise that there is no hope for some relationships. If a marriage must end, the counsellor is trained to help the couple to separate with less anger or bitterness and to reach a fair and friendly settlement of matters concerning their children and any property that they own.

In addition to Relate, counselling is provided by such organisations as Marriage Care (formerly the Catholic Marriage Advisory Council) and the Jewish Marriage Council. Your local Citizens Advice Bureau can also supply details of other similar organisations.

Lawyers may not always seem the most helpful people when a couple are splitting up as they do have a reputation for raising the temperature in divorce cases. However, this is not entirely deserved. There are some lawyers who do write letters and conduct cases in a manner that can only aggravate already explosive situations but the majority who specialise in family law are dedicated to keeping acrimony out of family disputes as much as possible. Details of lawyers in your locality who are members of the Solicitors Family Law Association can be obtained from the Law Society (see Appendix for the contact details).

Chapter 2:
Judicial separation and deeds of separation

In cases where, for some reason, the parties to a marriage do not wish to divorce or cannot do so, but wish to be legally separated, it is possible to obtain a decree of judicial separation. Examples of such cases might be where a husband or wife, or both, object to divorce on religious grounds, or where parents decide that they will remain legally married for the sake of the children, or for financial reasons.

To obtain a decree of judicial separation it is necessary to be able to prove one of the five facts on which irretrievable breakdown of marriage can be found. The facts are:

(a) adultery;

(b) desertion for a period of at least two years;

(c) unreasonable behaviour;

(d) two years' separation, with the consent of both parties;

(e) five years' separation, on the application of one of the parties, with no necessity for the consent of the other.

Under judicial separation decrees the courts have exactly the same powers as in divorce suits to make orders relating to matters concerning any children of the family, financial and property orders.

When a decree of judicial separation has been pronounced, the husband and wife are still legally married. Neither will be able to remarry. Because husbands and wives have not been divorced, they may still benefit under one another's pensions.

A decree of judicial separation can be converted into a divorce decree on the application of either of the parties, with the consent of the other. However, if a period of five years has elapsed since the date of separation, a husband or wife can apply for a judicial separation to be converted into a divorce decree without the consent of the other spouse.

Husbands and wives who have obtained decrees of judicial separation have no obligation to live with one another, even though they are still legally married.

Deeds of separation

Do not overlook the possibility of a trial separation, rather than opting for divorce immediately problems arise. Living apart from one another will give each of you the chance to think over your position and assess the importance of your spouse in your life.

Many couples who do not wish to divorce but have decided to live separately enter into separation agreements, which can be formalised by the creation of a legal deed.

On the breakdown of most relationships, there will be crucial questions to be resolved, particularly if you have children and/or property. It is important to give time and thought to what the future arrangements for the family are going to be.

Here again family mediation can help you to reach agreement. It is often very hard for couples to talk to one another in the emotional turmoil which the breakdown of a relationship produces. In mediation you will each have a chance to give your views and express your hopes for the future. You will be encouraged to speak to one another in a calm and neutral atmosphere, and to try to reach your own solutions to the matters which need to be decided. You make the decisions; the mediator is simply there to help you communicate with one another.

If you reach agreement, and many couples do, the terms of your agreement will be set out in writing. It is important to know that an agreement reached in mediation is not legally enforceable, however. Whether you reach agreement through mediation or by yourselves, it is a good idea to have a deed of separation drawn up by solicitors.

A legal deed of separation frees a husband and wife from the duty to live with one another. It sets out the terms of any decisions made about the children of the family, money or property.

It is extremely important to keep in mind that the terms set out in a deed of separation or other agreement between husband and wife can be overruled or amended by the court, should the parties decide to divorce.

The advantage of having a deed of separation, however, is that the courts will always look carefully at any agreement before considering making orders which will alter their provisions.

It is advisable to make sure that the husband and wife are advised by different solicitors before a deed of separation is prepared. This is to avoid any suggestion being made later that one person used undue influence over the other, in order to persuade him or her to agree to certain issues that are not in his or her interests.

The template deed of separation produced in the Appendix relates to the final terms of separation only; if necessary, you can agree interim terms and place those into an interim deed of separation if you wish. It would be prudent to at least obtain initial legal advice before proceeding to draw up a deed of separation, because otherwise the agreement may not be upheld in court.

Husbands and wives do not always enter into agreements on equal terms. The husband, or the wife, may be more financially aware than the other spouse. Occasionally, one will be a rather dominant person, accustomed to getting his or her own way, whilst the other will give in rather than face confrontation. In cases like this, the weaker party, if represented by a solicitor, will be able to negotiate a fairer settlement.

Where there is no suggestion of undue influence, the court will be slow to interfere with agreements entered into by competent adults who have been advised by solicitors, unless there has been a very significant change in the circumstances of the parties since the agreement was made.

Chapter 3:
Can you handle your own divorce?

Going through a divorce can be one of the most stressful experiences in life. It will affect you emotionally, financially and, of course, legally.

Your divorce will involve important legal decisions concerning:

(a) financial support

(b) division of property

(c) arrangements for your children under 16, or under 18 if still in school or learning a trade

Whilst these are vital issues, the law on these points is not particularly complex.

How does the divorce process work?

One person will start the proceedings leading to divorce by filling out a *Petition (Form D8)* and sending it and other documents to court. This person is the 'petitioner'.

The other spouse (the 'respondent') must respond to the petition, which states why the marriage should be ended using one of the five facts that prove that the marriage has irretrievably broken down.

In an amicable uncontested (or 'undefended'; this Guide uses the two terms interchangeably) divorce, the couple should discuss who will be the petitioner and who will be the respondent. There is no stigma attached to being the respondent nowadays, although it will necessitate admitting to one or more of the five facts of divorce. A respondent's behaviour does not necessarily affect the issues relating to property or children.

Any disputes or questions can slow the process down significantly. Therefore, it should be your aim to be reasonable in your demands and to agree on matters where possible at every stage. Chapter 15 takes you step-by-step through the divorce process. For a quick overview, see the 10-step overview to a simple, undefended divorce at the beginning of this Guide.

Do you need a solicitor?

To answer this question, ask yourself the following five questions:

(a) Is your divorce contested or uncontested?

If you and your spouse agree that you should divorce, your divorce is 'uncontested'. The vast majority of divorces are uncontested. You do not necessarily need a solicitor unless you disagree on other issues, such as the level of maintenance or the division of property.

If one spouse is unwilling to divorce, the divorce is 'contested' by that spouse. In this case, the services of a solicitor will be needed to determine whether there are grounds for divorce.

(b) Do you have minor children?

The most important issues in divorce are those involving the welfare of any children under 18 (known as minor children). These issues include child support, parental responsibility and orders for residence and contact (formerly known as 'custody' and 'access'). Because these issues are so important, the court will be concerned that what has been decided is in the best interests of the minor children.

Since the welfare and proper care of your children is paramount, you should ask a solicitor to approve the agreements concerning your children that you and your spouse have made. An experienced solicitor can guide you to a settlement that the court will approve for the children.

(c) Do you have property that can be divided easily?

If your divorce consists of deciding who, for example, keeps different items of furniture, you and your spouse should be able to resolve these questions without a solicitor. If you own substantial property, you will want a solicitor to ensure that you receive your full entitlement and that the division of property is tax-effective.

(d) Do you need or expect future support from your spouse?

If you expect to be financially dependent upon your spouse after the divorce, you may need a solicitor to help you negotiate maintenance and make the obligation binding by means of a court order.

(e) Are you sure you have proper grounds for a divorce?

Your rights to a divorce are not automatic. You must show one of the five facts that prove the legal requirements to obtain a divorce.

You probably do not need a solicitor if:

- you and your spouse both want the divorce and agree on the division of property;

- you have no minor children or you can agree about the arrangements for your children;

- your assets are not substantial;

- you are not disputing maintenance or child support;

- you are certain that you have proper grounds for divorce.

Even if you need a solicitor for financial matters, you can save yourself money by conducting the divorce yourself and by seeking to agree on matters with your spouse as much as possible.

Representing yourself

There are obvious benefits to handling your own divorce.

- Without a solicitor, you save legal fees. Solicitors charge by the hour so in complex cases the legal fees can become unaffordable.

- Without a solicitor, your divorce may be less adversarial. Solicitors can sometimes bring an adversarial atmosphere to a case that could be resolved more quickly and smoothly in an informal atmosphere involving only you and your spouse.

- Without a solicitor, your case may move faster. Your solicitor may be too busy with other cases, causing you needless delays.

One money-saving approach is to retain a solicitor to answer questions that may arise, rather than to represent you formally. This way you save legal fees and still have available to you the professional assistance you may need.

Finding a solicitor

Many solicitors handle divorce cases, and some specialise in family law. It should not be difficult to find one to advise you on your divorce and to answer your questions efficiently and economically. You can find a solicitor by:

- seeking referrals from friends or family members who have gone through a divorce;

- asking your local divorce court for the names of the more active divorce solicitors in your area. Similarly, a Citizens Advice Bureau may be an excellent referral source;

- calling the Law Society or the Solicitors Family Law Association. Both are listed in the Appendix.

A solicitor has a duty to advise you as to whether you are entitled to help with payment of your legal costs for your divorce and related matters, such as maintenance, questions relating to children or division of property. Whilst many solicitors do accept publicly funded (ex Legal Aid) work, others do not. Any solicitor should be willing to refer you to solicitors who do such work which is funded by the Community Legal Service.

What should you ask a solicitor?

Don't be afraid to interview any potential solicitor to be sure you feel comfortable with him or her. Your solicitor should be attentive and ask questions that indicate that he or she is listening to you.

Your questions should include the following:

- How long have you been in practice?

- Can you provide references?

- What percentage of your cases are divorce?

- Do you belong to the Solicitors Family Law Association?

- Do you generally represent the husband, the wife or both?

- Who within the office will handle the case? How much delegation will be involved?

- What will be the general approach to the case, and how long will it take?

- What approximate outcome might be expected?

- Approximately how much will it cost, what is your hourly rate, and how is the fee to be paid?

- Am I eligible for help with the payment of my legal fees?

Since one of the objectives of this book is to help you save money on your legal fees, here are a few ways to keep those costs to an absolute minimum:

(a) Do not hire a solicitor solely on the basis of reputation. A lesser known solicitor may be equally effective for a far lower fee.

(b) Use your time with the solicitor efficiently. Limit your telephone calls to him or her, and be concise when you do call. Keep a running list of specific questions you want to discuss the next time you call. The same rule applies to office visits.

(c) Give information to your solicitor's secretary whenever possible. It will save your solicitor's time.

(d) Ask for itemised bills, and review them carefully. Question anything you don't understand or that seems excessive, and expect clear explanations.

The Community Legal Service

Do you qualify for public funding help with the payment of your legal fees? Find out if you're eligible from the Legal Services Commission (formerly the Legal Aid Board) or a Citizens Advice Bureau.

If you qualify, the Legal Services Commission may pay your solicitor's fees in the form of a loan that must be repaid out of the proceeds of the financial settlement made with your spouse.

Chapter 4:
The grounds for divorce

You or your spouse may want to divorce, but you must satisfy certain legal requirements in order to qualify for a divorce.

- You must have been married for at least one year, and one of you must have resided in England or Wales for the year preceding the divorce, or consider England or Wales your principal place of residence.

- If you have been married for less than a year, you or your spouse can obtain a judicial separation or enter into a deed of separation until you have been married the required year, and then obtain a divorce.

- There is only one basic ground for divorce: the irretrievable breakdown of the marriage. Irretrievable breakdown is proved by establishing one or more of the following facts:

  Fact A: Adultery

  Fact B: Unreasonable behaviour

  Fact C: Desertion

  Fact D: Two-year separation with the consent of the other party (no fault)

  Fact E: Five-year separation when no consent is needed

Fact A: Adultery

You must prove that, through either admission or sufficient circumstantial evidence, your spouse had a sexual liaison with another person and that you find it intolerable to live with your spouse.

You can name the other person involved as a co-respondent, but it is not essential to do so, and can have serious consequences. It is usually best to avoid naming a co-respondent. If you wish to name the other person, you are best advised to discuss this first with a solicitor.

If this is an uncontested divorce and your spouse admits adultery, he or she can write an affidavit providing proof of adultery in the last six months. This record would become part of your court file, and the facts would be inserted into the petition as well.

If adultery is the fact to prove the ground for divorce, not more than six months must have elapsed from the time you became aware of your spouse's adultery, whether you are living together or separately.

Fact B: Unreasonable behaviour

You must show that your spouse has behaved in such a way that you cannot reasonably be expected to live with this person. There are many examples of unreasonable behaviour, but the following are commonly cited:

- Drinking

- Drug abuse

- Gambling

- Financial extravagance

- Refusing sex or excessive sexual demands

- Mental instability

- Nagging

- Insulting remarks

- Refusal to have children

- Sexual deviance

- Neglect

- No common shared interests

Unreasonable behaviour is now the most common fact on which to prove the ground for divorce.

Fact C: Desertion

Your spouse must have deserted you without your consent for a period of at least two years.

Fact D: Two-year separation

If, by consent, you and your spouse have lived apart for at least two years immediately preceding the presentation of the petition, and you both agree to a divorce, your separation can be grounds for divorce. This is sometimes referred to as no-fault divorce.

Living apart does not necessarily mean that you have to be in two different homes, if you are able to satisfy the court that you have been living separate lives under the same roof. This would usually mean eating meals separately, not going out together, and not doing any sort of housework – cooking, cleaning or ironing, for example – for one another.

If you are asking for a decree on the ground of two-year separation but have been living separately in this way under the same roof, you might be asked to come to the court to explain the circumstances.

Fact E: Five-year separation

If you and your spouse have lived apart for at least five years immediately preceding the date of the petition, you do not need the consent of your spouse in order to obtain a divorce.

Chapter 5: Mediation

Mediation has been used increasingly by divorcing couples in this country for more than 20 years. Over that period mediation services have become ever more skilled in helping divorcing or separating couples to make their own decisions about what should happen in relation to their children and finances.

The breakdown of any relationship is a traumatic business. We all invest a great deal, emotionally and materially, in marriage. It is hard to escape the feelings of bitterness and even betrayal so often associated with its breakdown.

Unfortunately, these feelings can be exacerbated by court proceedings. In addition, there can be an inevitable sense that the lawyers have taken over. Worse still, if disputes have to be settled by a court the decision may be one which is unacceptable to both sides and the expense of court hearings can be out of proportion to the reality of the dispute.

Mediation offers another way. Professionally trained mediators are completely neutral and non-directive. A husband and wife will each be given the time and opportunity to explain their individual problems. The couple will then be seen together and each will be helped to understand what the viewpoint of the other is. It is astonishing how often a couple are unable to talk to one another at all, let alone listen to what the other is trying to say.

The mediator will help them to realise where there are areas of agreement. Since every parent wants what is best for his or her child, that will be one thing on which both will be able to agree. From there, the areas of dispute will be identified. The mediator will encourage each spouse to suggest possible ways in which the dispute might be resolved. In financial disputes the mediator will help the couple to identify their assets and their needs, and then look at possible ways to arrive at a fair division.

Mediation is completely confidential, the only exception to this being where there is a disclosure of a risk to someone, particularly a child. The husband and wife are encouraged to report back to their solicitors about the progress of the mediation and any eventual proposals for agreement. The proposals reached will not be legally binding unless the solicitors take steps to have them made orders of the court.

The process of mediation empowers the spouses to reach their own decisions. If they can, this is of enormous benefit not only to themselves but, even more crucially, to their children. It takes the heat out of disagreement. Mediated agreements are likely to last longer than court orders. The fact that the parents have been able to agree about what should happen to the children means that they will find it easier to negotiate any changes to the agreement which may become necessary as time passes.

Compared with court proceedings, mediation is extremely cheap. If you do reach agreement, that agreement can be made into a court order by consent, without the necessity of anyone actually going to court to give evidence.

The names and addresses of mediation organisations which you can contact, including the charity National Family Mediation, are provided in the Appendix.

Chapter 6:
Protecting yourself during divorce

Not all divorces are amicable. If, during the divorce, your spouse acts unreasonably, you may need the powers of the court to:

   (a)   protect you and your children from violence;

   (b)   protect you and your children from harassment;

   (c)   protect your property;

   (d)   protect your income and financial security.

Protection from violence and harassment

See chapter 13 on domestic violence.

Protecting your property

It is not uncommon for one or both spouses going through divorce to conceal or hide assets to prevent them from being divided equitably by the court.

If you believe your spouse owns assets that he or she is attempting to transfer, conceal or put in trust, you may want the court to freeze those assets. In order to assist the court, gather as much information as possible concerning those assets, including their location. For example, it would help to have details of your spouse's bank account.

What can you do to protect your interest in a matrimonial home that is in the sole name of your spouse? To prevent your spouse from selling or mortgaging the property, you can put a 'restriction' against it on the land register.

You can find out if the property is registered by completing Form SIM. If the property is registered, you can place a restriction against it by completing Form MH1. Both forms are obtainable from the Land

Registry's website at www.landreg.gov.uk. If the property is unregistered, you must apply for a restriction to the Land Charges Department in Plymouth (see Appendix for their contact details). Contact them for advice on how to do it.

A word of caution: A restriction is not effective once a *Decree Absolute* is granted, as the home is no longer considered the 'matrimonial' home. Never seek a *Decree Absolute* until you are certain you will receive your fair share of the property.

If your spouse refuses to leave or sell the matrimonial home or consent to a divorce, Section 30 of the Law of Property Act allows the court to order the property to be sold. In such cases the court may decide to divide the property to the disadvantage of the unco-operative spouse.

What about changing the locks? You are not entitled to change the locks, even for your own protection, unless you have first obtained an exclusion order.

Protecting your financial security

Resolve as many matters as possible amicably, without a solicitor. It is always best to work out financial matters as quickly as possible following the decision to divorce. You and your spouse may be able to avoid interim court orders altogether if you understand and respect each other's positions and deal in utmost good faith. The alternative, wrangling in court, is emotional, expensive and time-consuming.

If your spouse continues to pay the mortgage or rent and provide for the family needs as before, no interim court action is necessary. However, if the supporting spouse discontinues support, the other spouse can apply to the court for financial relief once his or her *Petition for Divorce* is duly lodged. Because the court seeks to maintain the financial stability of both spouses, it usually orders the supporting spouse to pay temporary income ('maintenance pending suit') until long-term arrangements are resolved through the *Decree Absolute.*

It is important to apply for a 'maintenance pending suit', if necessary, as soon as possible after filing the petition, because it can take the court some time to allocate a hearing date. The judge can order payments backdated to the date of your petition, but in the interim you may find yourself without funds. Therefore do consider your social security entitlement.

It is not necessarily a good idea to live more simply than you are used to during the divorce. It can suggest to the court that you are quite capable of doing so permanently, and the court may order a correspondingly low level of maintenance. For your own benefit as well as to provide accurate information to the court, consider these guidelines:

- Keep a detailed budget of what you spend to maintain a normal lifestyle.

- Divide the expenses between you and the children wherever possible.

- Keep up with your financial commitments.

- If necessary, arrange for a loan during the divorce proceedings to be repaid from the proceeds of the divorce.

- Do not take liberties with your spouse's credit cards. If you hold cards in joint names, cancel them and apply for cards individually.

Interim appeals

If you are dissatisfied with an interim court order, your recourse is to appeal. However, an appeal against an interim order is unlikely to be successful. District judges enjoy enormous discretion, and unless there is an error in law or fact, the appeal courts are unlikely to interfere with the judgment of the district judge.

Nevertheless, either spouse can appeal against a district judge's interim court order concerning children or financial matters. If you choose to appeal, a notice of appeal must be filed within five working days of the judge's interim order.

The appeal will proceed from the district judges to the County court Circuit Judge or High Court Judge and, if there is a point of law involved, to the Court of Appeal. Occasionally, an appeal reaches the House of Lords.

An appeal against even an interim order is a serious matter and should not be undertaken frivolously. Moreover, an appeal is best handled by a solicitor, and can be expensive. Since the loser normally pays the legal fees for both sides, an appeal should be considered with caution.

Chapter 7:
Who gets what when you split up?

Questions about money and property tend to come up in almost every relationship breakdown. In some cases, of course, there is no problem. If two people have been married or living together, there is no property, they have no children, and each of them has a job, there should be no difficulties about finances or property when their relationship founders. However, in most relationships the financial facts are not so straightforward. For example, when only one partner has been in paid employment, with the other staying at home to care for their children throughout the relationship, or when they have been purchasing a house or flat on a mortgage, someone has to decide who gets what when they separate. It is a hard but inescapable fact that two households are not going to be able to live as cheaply as one did.

Even where two people have been living in rented accommodation, particularly if rented from the local authority, the tenancy can be an important asset and complications can arise.

If your marriage is breaking down, and you have decided to separate, the first step is to see whether you can agree between you over what is to happen about your finances and any property you may own. If you can't agree, you should definitely attempt to get help from a qualified mediator. Why? One good reason is that reaching agreement with the help of mediation will be much cheaper than asking the court to decide what should happen. Even if you are publicly funded, you may still have to meet the costs of lawyers and a court hearing in the end. However, if you can't even reach an agreement with the help of mediation, the law has to be the last resort. (See chapter 5 for an explanation of the mediation process.)

It used to be the case that if a married woman owned any property or earned any money, it belonged to her husband. It was not until late in the 19th century that the law began to give a wife some rights over her own finances. Today, husbands and wives are on equal terms when decisions have to be made about income and property rights on divorce. A court can order that one partner – usually the husband, but it could be the wife – should make regular payments for the maintenance of the other. Orders can also be made for the division of any capital assets, such as houses, flats, savings or pension entitlements.

A spouse who has not actually filed a divorce petition can still apply to the court for a maintenance order if the other spouse should be supporting him or her and is refusing to do so.

Since the introduction of the child support law in 1993, decisions about maintenance to be paid for most children are made by the Child Support Agency (CSA).

What are your rights to money and property if your marriage ends?

When a marriage has broken down the court has the power to make any orders about finances or property which seem to the court to be just, including maintenance orders.

This means that the court can make orders affecting property or other capital assets which one or both spouses may own. In most cases, of course, the most important asset which a couple has is the home in which they have lived together.

That home may have been purchased in the sole name of the husband. He alone may have provided the deposit when it was purchased, and have paid off the instalments on the mortgage entirely from his own earnings. He may have other capital assets, savings in a building society, for example, or a car, or own his own business and have a great deal of capital invested in that. He may have a substantial entitlement to a pension to which he has contributed over many years.

Less often, the wife may be wealthy in her own right, owning property or valuable jewellery, for example. She could be a successful businesswoman or a professional woman with capital assets, substantial savings or a pension entitlement.

The court will look at every bit of property or capital owned by the husband or the wife. Each must complete a document which gives a comprehensive account of his or her financial position – *Financial Statement Form E* (see pages 177–96). The court then looks at the facts of the particular marriage to help it decide what orders it can make which will be fair to everyone. When it does so, it has to keep in mind that if there are any children of the marriage, the interests of those children will be the most important consideration. This often means that the parent with children living with him or her will be more likely to keep the home, at least until the children have all finished their full-time education.

What does the court take into account?

When a divorce court has to make decisions about money or property ('ancillary matters' as they are called), there are certain things that must be taken into account by law. If the judge should make an order about money or property without giving proper consideration to these matters, the order would be appealable.

(a) Resources

Resources include the income of the husband and of the wife, the earning capacity which each of them has, and any property or other assets. It is important to remember that, in considering earning capacity, the court does not simply look at what each partner is earning at the time when the matter comes before it. Often, the wife will not have been earning money for some years because she has been looking after young children. If the children are now at school, for example, the judge might decide that the mother has skills which give her an earning capacity, even it is only to be on a part-time basis. If the mother happened to have some qualification, in teaching or nursing perhaps, that would be taken into account. Alternatively, it might be possible for her to undergo some training to improve the skills which she already has in order to get her into the job market again.

The court will always look at all the facts. A mother who has not been in employment for 20 years will not be expected to go straight out and earn her own living. The ages of her children will be an important consideration; the state of the job market in her locality will also be taken into account.

Case study

Sharon and Ken are divorcing after nine years of marriage. They have two young children, who will be living with Sharon. They have always lived in rented accommodation and neither of them has any substantial capital or savings. Shortly after they separated, Ken's wealthy aunt died, leaving him £100,000, which he will receive in the near future. Can Sharon expect to be awarded some of that money by the court?

The answer is that in all those circumstances it is likely that Sharon would be given a lump sum by the court to be paid by Ken from his inheritance. That £100,000 is a resource which he is certain to have in the foreseeable future; it can consequently be brought into consideration by the court.

On the other hand, had Ken's wealthy aunt been a woman still in her fifties and in excellent health, the court would not have taken Ken's prospect of an inheritance from her into account. She might not have left him anything at all in her will and she might have continued to live for another 30 years or more.

Case study

Julie and Tim are divorcing after 11 years of marriage. They have no children. Tim has always been the breadwinner whilst Julie stayed at home as a housewife throughout the marriage. Julie is asking for maintenance. Since their separation a few months ago, Julie has been doing a course in book-keeping. She is doing well on the course and expects to qualify as a book-keeper in six months' time. The court will take into account that Julie can reasonably be expected to obtain her book-keeping qualification and then find a job so that she can support herself. If the court is satisfied that book-keeping jobs will be available within a reasonable distance of where Julie will be living, an order for Tim to pay her maintenance may well take account of the situation by providing for the payments to be made only for a certain length of time, say 12 months, to give Julie a chance to get on her feet and become self-supporting.

Every case is unique, of course, and there are many other important considerations for the court in each one, so that Sharon, Ken, Julie and Tim can only be examples of what might happen.

(b) Needs, obligations and responsibilities

Once the court has determined the resources of a husband and wife, the needs, obligations and responsibilities of each have to be taken into account. The most obvious need for anyone is some sort of roof over his or her head. The court will do its utmost to ensure that both spouses have a home at the end of the day.

Desirable as it is for each of the divorcing partners to have a home, this cannot always be achieved. If there are children of the family, the court will always give priority to providing a home for them. This means that the parent with whom the children are to live will almost always be the one who will be allowed to remain in the former matrimonial home when there is not enough money to provide two homes.

Because the mother is often, although not by any means always, the parent with whom the children will live, it is often the mother who stays in the matrimonial home. This has given rise to a view, fairly common among fathers, that the courts favour mothers when it comes to financial matters in divorce proceedings.

In fact, the courts try to be as fair as possible, whilst remaining mindful that the needs of any children have to come first. In some cases, the mother will be allowed to remain in the home with the children but only until they leave full-time education. At that stage, the court may decide that the home should be sold and the proceeds of the sale divided as the court considers just.

It cannot be stated too often that every case has its own individual set of facts. This means that it is impossible to be certain about what may or may not happen in any particular case. There are so many factors to be taken into account that the best that can be attempted is 'an educated guess'.

(c) Contributions

The court must take into account the contributions to the marriage made by each spouse. The husband may have made all the financial contributions; some think that, because of that, their wives should not be entitled to claim anything.

However, in many marriages where the husband has been the sole earner and contributor of money, the wife has played her part by bringing up the children, cleaning, washing, ironing and cooking for the family, and generally carrying out all the work lumped together as 'being a housewife'.

The courts have come round to the view that the sort of contribution made by a wife who stays at home to care for the home, the husband and their children is equally important as that of the man who goes out and earns the money.

(d) Age

The ages of the husband and wife can affect the decision of the court about financial matters.

Case study

Doreen, a 55-year-old wife, has stayed at home caring for her family for 35 years. She has never had any training which would equip her for a job outside the home. Her husband, Frank, who is the same age, preferred to have his wife making things comfortable for him at home whilst he built up his own profitable business, from the proceeds of which he has supported Doreen and their children. It will be difficult, if not impossible, for Frank to persuade the court that Doreen ought to go out and get a job and be self-supporting to relieve him of the liability to provide for her in the future.

It has been said by the courts that 'marriage is not a meal ticket for life'. Although this reflects the court's hope that partners to a broken marriage can eventually become financially independent of one another, judges are realists. Women of 55, out of the job market for 35 years and with no special qualifications or skills, are not likely to be able to find jobs in today's conditions.

Doreen has made her contribution to the marriage over the years. Unless Frank is in a financial position to pay her a large sum of money to compensate her for loss of maintenance in the future, his liability to maintain her would be likely to continue.

The length of the marriage is important too.

Case study

Ben is a millionaire. He meets Audrey, who has no money at all. They marry, but very quickly realise that the marriage is a mistake and separate after only a year. There are no children. Can Audrey expect substantial financial provision from Ben?

The answer will almost certainly be 'no', although Audrey might get an order for maintenance for a limited period if she needs time to find a job.

(e) Is behaviour taken into account?

People are in a very vulnerable state at the time of the breakdown of their relationship. Often, extremely hurtful things are said and done, because when you are hurt yourself you usually feel like giving as good as you get. The husband, the wife or even both may behave in quite outrageous ways. When money and property cases come before the court, it is sometimes difficult for people to resist the temptation to tell the court all about the rotten behaviour of the other person. Husbands or wives often seem to believe that a partner's bad behaviour should affect the amount of money to be awarded by the court.

The court, however, is only allowed to take conduct into account in a very limited way. The behaviour must be so bad that any reasonable person would say that it would be unjust for the court to ignore it. This standard is a high one, and it means that only in a very few cases will the behaviour of one of the spouses be taken into account when it comes to deciding on a division of money or property.

In one particular case the wife had actually assisted the husband's suicide attempts because she was hoping to benefit financially on his death. At the same time, and unknown to him, she had been committing adultery. This behaviour was found by the court to satisfy the test, and the wife's entitlement to financial provision was reduced because of it.

Yet in another case, where a wife had been committing adultery with a boy half her age who was a guest in the matrimonial home, the judge decided that the wife's behaviour was not bad enough for him to take it into account when deciding financial matters.

(f) All the circumstances

The matters listed above are just some of the important things which the court must take into account when deciding financial and property cases in divorce; they are by no means the only things which will be considered. The law is that the judge must take into account all the circumstances in any particular case; as every case is unique, this means that advising on financial matters in divorce is not at all an easy task.

Also, remember that judges are human beings, with their own, very often unconscious, prejudices and opinions. The vast majority of them are skilled professionals, dedicated to being as fair as they can be to both parties in any case that comes before them. This does not mean, however, that there is only one obvious outcome to every case.

Reaching agreement without going to court

It is quite impossible for anyone to be absolutely certain of what the court will decide when presented with a particular set of facts and circumstances. It is therefore vitally important for you to think very carefully about whether you can possibly come to an agreement about your money and property when you divorce. This avoids the uncertainty, the delay – and the considerable expense! – of a court hearing.

Agreements have another advantage. It is unlikely that either the husband or wife will get exactly what he or she has been hoping for when an agreement is reached. However, even if both of them have been a little disappointed, at the same time they have arrived at a compromise which each is prepared to accept.

Once you go through the door of the court you are completely at the mercy of what the judge will decide. The judge's decision may be utterly devastating in its effect, on one side or the other. It can be, and surprisingly often is, a decision about which neither party is particularly happy.

Expert assistance in reaching agreement without court proceedings is available through various mediation organisations. Professionally trained, and absolutely neutral, mediators will not tell you what to do but will enable you to talk to each other and arrive at the solution that seems best to you. The fees charged involve couples in much less expense than the costs of a battle in court. More importantly, the process is much less emotionally stressful than an appearance in court, which most people find a huge ordeal. See chapter 5 for further information.

Some orders which the court can make

There are several types of order which the court can make in divorce proceedings. The most common orders are given below:

(a) Maintenance orders

These order that one spouse should make maintenance, or periodical payments (usually from the husband to the wife). Payments are normally ordered on a weekly or monthly basis. They can be limited to a set period. For example, in the case where Julie was training to become a book-keeper (see page 30), the court might order Tim to make periodical payments to her for a period of only 12 months.

It is the hope and the aim of the courts that husbands and wives will eventually become financially independent of one another, so that the 'meal ticket for life' situation does not arise. Yet in the case of Doreen and Frank (see page 32), it is not always possible for the court to take the view that someone is capable of achieving financial independence.

If a husband fails to make payments under a court order, enforcement proceedings can be taken in the court where the order was made. If the husband is in employment, it is possible to obtain an attachment of earnings order to ensure that his employers deduct the amount he should be paying from his wages and then pay it directly to his wife.

If, for some reason, it is not possible to obtain an attachment of earnings order, a husband who persistently fails to comply with a court order for maintenance could eventually be sent to prison.

Maintenance orders can be varied if there is a change in circumstances. If the husband loses his job, for example, he can apply to vary the payments downwards. If a wife has a part-time job and loses it, she can apply for a variation to increase the maintenance order.

(b) Lump sum orders

The court can order a husband or wife to make a payment of a lump sum of money to the other party. This sum can be of any amount, depending upon the assets of the parties in any particular case. A lump sum can be ordered in addition to maintenance payments, or it can be in final settlement of the financial obligations of the payer.

(c) Transfers of property

The court can order a husband or wife to transfer any property which belongs to that person to the other spouse. This order is often made when the property to be transferred is the spouse's interest in the former matrimonial home. In the particular circumstances of a case, it may be decided by the court that, for example, the wife should have the husband's share of a jointly owned home transferred to her.

These orders can be made in relation to all forms of property, including tenancies and company shares, for example.

Pensions and divorce

In dealing with financial aspects of divorce in the past, little if any attention may have been given to any pension entitlement which one partner (usually the husband) might have, particularly in cases where some years would have to pass before such a pension became payable. It has now been recognised that in many marriages the husband's pension entitlement can be one of the most important capital assets, sometimes worth even more than the matrimonial home.

As has already been said, it is now recognised by the courts that the contributions made by a wife as mother and homemaker are to be taken into account just as those made by a husband who has been the sole breadwinner. By making her contribution, the wife will have, indirectly, contributed towards the pension expectations of the husband.

For this reason the court can now take into account pension entitlement, just as with other assets of the spouses, and has the power to allocate proportions of that entitlement between them as it considers just in all the circumstances.

Compiling information

Organisation will help you cope with the financial matters of divorce and will serve you well as you embark on your new life. Keep careful records right from the outset of the divorce proceedings, and maintain them. You may be asked sometime during the divorce to disclose your full financial history. You will also need your spouse's complete financial history.

Assets

Make certain every important asset you and your spouse own is accounted for. It is remarkably easy to overlook valuable assets.

Use the following list to help.

- A valuation of the matrimonial home

- The redemption figure for the mortgage(s)

- Pension and other retirement plans

- Life insurance policies and surrender values

- Endowment policies and surrender values

- Pre- or post-nuptial agreements

- Bank statements for the past 12 months

- Building society passbooks for the past 12 months

- Share portfolios

- Accounts for the past 12 months if you are self-employed

- Wage slips for the past 12 months if you are an employee

- Details of any company directorships

- Tax returns for the past three years

- Credit card statements for the past 12 months

- Details of your liabilities

- Inventory of home contents (e.g. antiques, jewellery, art)

- Cash at bank, building society

- Savings accounts, including TESSAs, PEPs and ISAs

- Investments

- Motor vehicles

- Valuation of any other property

- Beneficial interests in trusts

- Inheritances

- A safe deposit box inventory

Do either you or your spouse own a business? If so, you should also have records of the following:

- Business plans

- Current accounts

- Life insurance policies maintained by the company that name either of you as beneficiary

- Tax returns of the business

Estimate the value of each item as accurately as possible. Indicate in which name each asset is held (i.e. in your name, in your spouse's name, jointly with your spouse or in trust). Also note the respective shares of jointly owned assets. Finally, list any borrowings or encumbrances against each asset to determine the equity to be divided.

Liabilities

Repeat this exercise for your liabilities:

- Mortgages

- Tax liabilities

- Hire purchase agreements

- Unsecured loans

- Charge account balances

- Credit card balances

- Child maintenance from previous marriages

- Personal guarantees

- Outstanding judgments

- Potential or threatened claims

Compile your records so you understand fully everything about your finances and those of your spouse.

Preparing a budget

Next, prepare details of expenditures or a budget of what it will cost you to live in a style reasonably similar to that which you enjoyed during the marriage. Include the following:

- Mortgage (including life assurance if it is an endowment mortgage)

- Utility charges (e.g. gas, electricity, water)

- Council Tax

- Food

- Car and travel costs (e.g. insurance, road tax, depreciation, AA/RAC membership)

- Clothes for yourself and your children

- Home contents insurance

- Buildings insurance

- Medical insurance

- School fees

- Entertainment and holidays

- Miscellaneous (e.g. newspapers, hairdresser, dry cleaner, personal items)

Form E

Form E has to be filed with the court if you are asking for any orders about property, income or pensions. A blank copy of this form is printed at the end of the book. As you will see, it asks many complex, detailed and perhaps rather daunting questions.

Unless your financial position is extremely simple, you should really get help in completing this form. A qualified family mediator or solicitor will be able to advise you.

So far as the page on pension entitlement is concerned, it is a good idea to photocopy this page and send it to your pension provider. Pension providers are under an obligation to provide all the details required without charge on the first request. Make sure you do not have to come back with more requests, because the providers can then charge for the additional information. It is for this reason that it is best to send them a full copy of the questions to be completed by them.

Chapter 8:
Children and the law

In an ideal world, the two most important people in the life of any child should be his or her mother and father. Sadly, today more and more children are being brought up by single parents, by a parent and step-parent, or even without either of their parents, in the care of a local authority. Millions of children have experienced parental separation. One half of those will have lost all contact with the non-resident parent within three years of the separation. Many children suffer the breakdown of carers' relationships more than once during their childhood and adolescence.

Before the Children Act was introduced, when parents divorced, even when they had come to a sensible agreement themselves about the future of their children, divorce law insisted that the court still had to make an order. It was almost as though the law believed that if your marriage had broken down, you could not be trusted to make decisions about your own children.

Parents who could not agree had to battle in court over 'custody' and 'access'. Some parents looked upon custody as ownership. Courts tried to make it clear that the parent without custody was just as important to the child, but the message was definitely not getting through. Warring parents refused to look on a custody order as anything but a matter of winning or losing. All too often the parent with custody would behave as though the other could be excluded from the child's life. Every request for access meant a further skirmish in the battle and often another fight in court. Once again, the real casualties would be the children.

Changes in the law

In past generations children were very much the property of their parents. The law would enforce the 'rights' of parents over their children.

The parents might be good, caring and loving, or bad, neglectful and abusive. It was only in the most extreme cases of cruelty that the law would interfere with the way in which children were treated. The changing pattern of adult relationships, with so many marriages breaking down, has been a major factor in the increasing involvement of the law with children.

Not all that long ago, it was only the father who had rights; the mother had none. A mother who had committed adultery would often be refused any future contact with her child by the court.

As a case example, in 1878, Harriet's mother had left her father for very good reasons. Yet the father took Harriet and her brothers and sisters away from their mother with the full approval of the court. The eldest child was only 12. The father could not look after them himself so boarded them out with 'clergymen and other persons ... in many and various places'. Their mother was only allowed to visit them once a month; all letters between the children and their mother were censored. Harriet was a brave child: when she was sixteen she wrote to the judge begging to be allowed to live with her mother, or at least to spend a holiday with her. 'Father has no place to take me to, and with one exception has never spent a vacation with us in over four years. I am almost always among strangers. I am longing to see some of my relations,' she wrote. But the court decided that it had no power to interfere with the father's legal right to absolute control over his children.

Contrast what happened to poor Harriet and her mother with what happened almost exactly a hundred years later, when Mrs Victoria Gillick, mother of five daughters, attempted to persuade a court that advice on contraception should not be given to them without her agreement whilst they were under the age of 16. The House of Lords decided that Mrs Gillick did not have complete control over her children. The rights of a parent come from the parent's duty to protect the child but the child has rights too. As he or she grows older, more intelligent and mature, his or her rights increase and the rights of the parents diminish.

The Children Act

One of the aims of the Children Act was to give children a voice. Another was to replace the old concepts of custody and access, old-fashioned legal words which had become so emotive, by the more neutral terms 'residence' and 'contact'.

Case study

William's mother has obtained a residence order from the court which provides that he should live with her. William's father has been granted a contact order, setting out the periods which William will spend with him. But these orders do not in any way lessen the parental responsibility of William's father, who can exercise it in any way he thinks best in William's interests, whenever William is visiting him. Moreover, William's father must be consulted about important decisions in the child's life — where he should go to school, for example.

The emphasis has completely shifted from parental 'rights' to parental responsibility.

The checklist

First, the welfare of the child is paramount in deciding any question about the child. Delay is prejudicial to the child's welfare. Attention must be paid to the following matters, set out in the Act and called the checklist:

(a) The ascertainable wishes and feelings of the child, considered in the light of his or her age and understanding.

(b) The physical, emotional and educational needs of the child.

(c) The likely effect upon the child of any change of circumstances.

(d) The age, sex, background and other relevant characteristics of the child.

(e) Any harm that the child has suffered or which the child may be at risk of suffering.

(f) How capable each of the parents and any other relevant person is of meeting the child's needs.

(g) The range of powers available to the court.

The child's wishes and feelings

Family lawyers know that the wishes and feelings of almost every child involved in court proceedings when parents are in conflict are sadly predictable. Most children, asked to name a wish, will say that they want their parents to be together again, without any arguments. Unfortunately, this is one wish that a judge cannot grant.

If the judge takes the view that not to make an order would be better for the child concerned, then the court does not have to make an order at all. From the viewpoint of the child, it is a much better and happier option to know that his or her parents have decided what is to happen together, rather than have to deal with an almighty court battle taking place, with an order being made which will leave one parent the 'winner' and the other the 'loser'.

Chapter 9:
Caring for the children

When parents split up, their children are in the front line. If the children are of an age where they still need parental care, the first question to be answered is where and with whom they are going to live. Tied up with that decision are the questions about how often and for how long they will see the parent with whom they are not living.

Any breakdown in a relationship is going to be traumatic for the couple concerned. If they have been sufficiently committed to one another to have children, it is almost inevitable that the trauma of the breakdown will be correspondingly greater. Far too often children get caught in the crossfire because parents are too preoccupied with their own feelings of hurt and rejection to think clearly.

No loving parent would willingly inflict emotional pain on a child, but when trying to cope with the turmoil of separation and loss a parent can be blinded to what should be obvious.

Children have a right to know

Children, even very young children, are only too aware of any tension in the relationship between their parents. The story is told of the couple who resolved that their small son and daughter would never be given a hint of any disagreement between them. When they were irritated with one another they took particular care to be even more polite than usual. They prided themselves on their success in concealing their quarrels until the day when they had to use force to separate their squabbling children. The little boy pointed at his sister and said accusingly: 'She called me 'darling' first!'

This story illustrates precisely what so often happens. Parents may believe that their children have no idea that there are any problems between them but it is in fact rare for children of a floundering relationship not to realise that one or both of their parents is feeling unhappy, or that something is wrong.

Some parents find the temptation to enlist the sympathy of the children irresistible but most children love their parents equally. Children certainly need both parents. The fact that the parental relationship has broken down should not mean that they lose out any more than they must.

Parents who have decided to separate should try to explain to their children exactly what is happening. If at all possible they should explain to the children together. The words they use will obviously depend upon the ages of the children, but even the smallest children deserve to be given some explanation that they can understand.

Child psychiatrists who have made a study of the children of divorced or separated parents have come up with some surprising conclusions. For example, they have discovered that children often believe that the breakdown in their parents' relationship is somehow their fault. It needs to be carefully explained to a child that adults do stop loving one another sometimes. Equally, it should be emphasised that both parents still love the child and will not stop doing so whatever happens.

Child experts have also found that if a parent leaves home and there is no careful explanation given to young children, they will worry desperately about the possibility that the parent who is still there will vanish too. The child's reasoning is: if daddy can go away, so might mummy. Who will look after me then?

That might seem laughable to an adult, but for the child who does not understand what has happened or why, and to whom no one attempts to explain what has happened, the logic is remorseless.

Small children can feel great anxiety about the parent who leaves. Where will he or she sleep? Who will cook their meals? If there is no discussion about the parent's plans, the child may experience acute and quite unnecessary concern; this will be in addition to the unavoidable distress caused by the breakdown itself. Being able to visit the place where the absent parent will be living helps the child to come to terms with the new situation.

Some parents feel that talking to their children about the breakdown of their relationship is simply too difficult but if the children are given no explanation of what is happening in their lives, they are likely to be very frightened and confused.

Fortunately, there are now many organisations that offer counselling to parents at times like this. This counselling is called 'conciliation', but parents should not be put off by this word. It is often mistakenly thought to mean 'reconciliation', in other words an attempt to patch up a failed relationship. Conciliation recognises that the relationship has broken down. Counsellors work with the parents to find the best solutions to the practical problems thrown up by the breakdown.

Custody, care and control, and access

Before the Children Act was introduced, most people were familiar with the ideas of custody, care and control, and access. Orders could be made giving sole custody to one parent or joint custody to both, with care and control to one. Joint custody orders were not all that common, since the court had to be convinced that the parents could work together harmoniously for the good of their child before such an order would be made. More usual were orders giving sole custody, care and control to one parent.

In either case the parent who did not have care and control could be granted access – visiting access or staying (overnight) access, or both. In rare cases a parent would not be given access or would have access limited to sending letters, cards and gifts for birthdays and Christmas.

'Custody', 'care' and 'control' were emotive words. The non-custodial parent frequently felt excluded from a child's life. The word 'access' appeared to imply that the child somehow 'belonged' to the parent with care and control. The word 'custody' seemed to confirm that idea.

The mere fact that whenever a divorce took place there had to be a court order about what should happen to the children often gave rise to difficulties where there should have been none. For example, it was not unusual for sensible separating parents to be in complete agreement about what should happen in relation to their children. However, the court still had to intervene by making an order, even though it would be expressed as 'by consent'.

There was always some confusion about the extent of the right of the non-custodial parent to be consulted about important decisions in the life of a child – which school the child should attend, for example, whether the child should have a hospital operation, or which religion should be taught. Where parents were not on the best of terms following a split, the tendency might be for the custodial parent to make all the decisions without consulting the other parent at all. This behaviour would inevitably upset the other parent and, of course, the child. A parent like this was, consciously or unconsciously, using the child as a weapon in an ongoing conflict with the other parent.

Courts tried to give guidance, insisting that a custody order did not give the custodial parent absolute rights over all decision-making about the child. Attempts were sometimes made to overcome the problem by granting joint custody orders to emphasise the shared responsibility of the parents. However, most judges would only agree to joint custody orders when they were satisfied that the parents could relate to one another reasonably and make joint decisions. Therefore, in the most acrimonious cases, it was more likely that a sole custody order would be made, giving one parent the power to use the child as a pawn in the continuing warfare.

For all these reasons, custody orders were abolished, to be replaced by the – hopefully neutral – residence orders. Old orders are still in existence, however, although they will disappear with time.

New words for old?

Experts agree that the children of separated parents, each of whom encourages them to love the other, survive the breakdown of their parents' relationships best.

Laws cannot be passed to compel parents to be civil to one another, to put their own hurts aside and to encourage their children to love the parent who may have behaved badly as a partner, but it was realised that the orders made before the Children Act were actually working against parental co-operation, in that they implied that one parent had 'won' and the other 'lost'. The very words custody and access had become loaded with emotive overtones.

The thinking behind the Act was to try to avoid this kind of unnecessary emotional distress for parents, and their children, as far as possible. The emphasis has now been placed firmly on the concept of parental responsibility. Each parent is equally responsible whenever the child is with that parent.

The choices for the court

The court now has three choices when faced with the problem of what should happen to the children on the breakdown of a marriage:

(a) To make no order at all

This is now the preferred option, one which was not open to the court prior to the introduction of the Children Act. It underlines the fact that it is the parents who are responsible. Parents are obviously the best people to decide matters about their child. If they can do so, it is right that the decisions should be left to them and that the court does not intervene. Children are much happier too if they feel that their parents have come to joint decisions.

(b) To make a residence order in favour of one parent and a contact order in favour of the other

Unfortunately, when parents cannot agree, it has to be admitted that this kind of order will all too often be seen by them in the old winning/losing terms. The mere change of wording seldom helps in reality. If there is a court battle as a result of which one parent gains a residence order, it matters little to the other parent that the order is no longer expressed as custody, care and control.

(c) To make a split residence order

This is an order which means that the child is to reside with one parent for part of the week, month or year, and with the other for the remainder of the week, month or year. Judges may be tempted to make such orders to avoid giving the win/lose impression, but these orders are unusual. The problem with a split residence order is that it is generally better for a child to know where his or her home is. Dividing the child's time more or less equally between the parents can result in a lack of security and permanence for the child, whatever the satisfaction for the parents.

Other orders the court can make

(a) Prohibited steps orders

These orders are made when the court wants to limit the parental responsibility of a parent in some specific way.

Case study

Sarah and Tom are the divorced parents of Luke. A residence order has been made in Sarah's favour. Luke attends a school near his home with Sarah. The school does not accept a certain style of haircut and will exclude any boy with that hairstyle. Luke is going to have weekend staying contact with Tom, who has told Sarah that he intends to exercise his parental responsibility by having Luke's hair cut in the style banned by the school. Sarah can apply to the court for a prohibited steps order, forbidding Tom to exercise his parental responsibility by having Luke's hair cut in that particular style.

(b) Specific issue orders

These orders are made when there is some specific matter of dispute between parents which they cannot resolve by agreement.

Case study

Tom has come to the conclusion that Luke's school is run by a reactionary and authoritarian head teacher. He wants Luke to change to another local school, where hairstyles are a matter of choice. Sarah, on the other hand, is happy with Luke's present school and wishes him to continue there. Either Sarah or Tom can apply to the court to decide on the question of which school Luke should attend. This kind of application results in a specific issue order when the court settles the dispute, although it is to be hoped that parents can resolve this sort of disagreement between themselves, without having to apply to the court.

Who may apply for orders?

(a) Residence, contact, prohibited steps or specific issue orders

   (a)   Any parent can apply.

   (b)   Any guardian can apply.

   (c)   Any person with a residence order can apply.

(b) Residence or contact orders only

   (a)   Anyone listed under 1 above.

   (b)   Anyone married to the parent of a child, who has treated the child as 'a child of the family', has the right to apply, even if the marriage has ended.

   (c)   Anyone with whom a child has lived for a period of at least three years.

   (d)   Anyone who has the consent of each person with a residence order in respect of the child.

   (e)   If the child is in the care of a local authority, anyone with the consent of the local authority can apply.

   (f)   In any other case, each person with parental responsibility for a child can apply.

(c) Other people

Anyone not entitled to make an application under any of the categories set out above may apply to the court for permission to make an application. This includes the child, who may be granted permission if he or she is considered to be of sufficient understanding and maturity.

Grandparents, and other interested relatives or friends of the child, can also apply for permission to make an application, if they do not qualify under one of the categories listed above. There will usually be little difficulty in obtaining permission for anyone who can show that it would be in the interests of a child for an order to be made.

The effect of residence orders

Changing a child's surname

If you are considering changing the surname of your child, you should be aware that it is an automatic condition of all residence orders that you must get the written consent of every person with parental responsibility for the child, or the permission of the court, before you can do so. In certain circumstances, the court will give permission for a child's surname to be changed, even where one of the child's parents is opposed to the change.

Changing a child's surname is not something that should be done lightly. A court would need to be satisfied that the change is going to be in the interests of the child.

Case study

Gemma R's parents divorced and her mother remarried when Gemma was four years old. The new husband is Mr T. Her mother allowed Gemma to be known as Gemma T by friends and neighbours, and registered her at school as 'Gemma R known as T'. Mr R objected to his daughter being known by her stepfather's surname. Gemma's mother applied to the court for leave to change the child's surname.

It was decided that it would not be in Gemma's interests, and would be totally unrealistic, for the court to make an order forbidding the use of the mother's new surname by Gemma. The order would be impossible to enforce. Gemma knew that her real surname was R, but her friends and schoolteachers called her Gemma T. The court held that it would not be in her interests to have the name by which she was already known changed to her real name.

This case was decided in the early 1980s. Although one can understand the reasoning behind the decision, it should not be taken as an encouragement to mothers to defy the law, which now makes it clear that a child's surname may not be changed without the consent of the other parent or the leave of the court.

A change of surname is a question on which a child might have views of his or her own. In such a case, if the child were to be of sufficient maturity and understanding, the court might grant leave for the child to make an application about a change of surname.

Taking a child out of the country

Where a residence order is in force, no person may remove the child from the UK without either the written consent of every person with parental responsibility or the permission of the court.

However, a person who has a residence order may remove the child for a period of less than one month. This is to enable people with residence orders to take children abroad for the purpose of normal holidays.

It sometimes happens that the non-resident parent suspects that the parent with the residence order plans to take the child abroad permanently, rather than simply for a holiday. In such a case, the anxious parent can apply for a prohibited steps order, forbidding removal of the child by the other parent.

Conditions attached to orders

If the court considers it to be in the interests of a child, it can attach a condition or conditions to a residence order. For example, if the judge thought that there was a real risk of a parent with residence taking the child abroad permanently, the court could attach a condition to the residence order to minimise the risk. The condition may be that the parent with residence was not to remove the child from the jurisdiction for any period without the permission of the court or the consent of the other parent.

Family assistance orders

Behind all the provisions of the Children Act lies the hope that parents will be able to co-operate with one another for the sake of their children. Lawyers and other professionals concerned with families are only too aware of the strength of feeling that exists when relationships which were once loving have broken down.

Sometimes it is just too much to expect that emotions will cool immediately when disputes have had to be resolved by court proceedings. The win/lose view is likely to persist. The temptation to use the children as weapons in the ongoing conflict between the parents can seem irresistible but it can have disastrous results for the children.

For this reason, the courts have power to make family assistance orders. These orders require that a person, such as a local authority social worker, should 'advise, assist and (where appropriate) befriend any person named in the order'. Social workers have had rather a bad press in recent years; parents sometimes become alarmed by the suggestion that a social worker should be involved with their family. However, in the case of family assistance orders, social workers are there to do just that – assist. Their training enables them to sort out areas of difficulty.

People who may be named in a family assistance order are:

(a)   any parent;

(b)   any guardian;

(c)   any person with whom the child is living;

(d)   any person in whose favour a contact order is in force;

(e)   any child.

These orders are only made if the court takes the view that the circumstances of the case are 'exceptional'. The court must also be satisfied that the consent of every person named in the order (other than the child) has been obtained in order to make the order.

Family assistance orders are intended to be a temporary help in situations where parents or other interested parties find it difficult to communicate directly with one another in the interests of the child with whom they are all concerned. They are made for periods of six months.

Families with communication difficulties can also seek help from family mediation services. Your local Citizens Advice Bureau or telephone directory will provide addresses. Also see the list of addresses in the Appendix.

Does the mother always get the children?

Family lawyers are frequently asked this question when there is a dispute between parents about with whom their children should live. Fathers often believe that they are at a disadvantage when a court makes this kind of decision.

Parents do start off, so far as the law is concerned, on equal terms. There is no particular magic in being a mother when it comes to a battle over residence. Every child is an individual, with his or her own set of characteristics and circumstances. The court will do its utmost to ensure that the decision made about any particular child will be in that child's best interests.

That means taking account of all the circumstances. One factor that cannot be ignored is that, in most cases, it is often considered that a baby or a very young child will be more adequately cared for by a mother than by a father.

Again, this is not true of all babies or very young children. Many modern fathers are equally capable of caring for their children from babyhood and some mothers do not provide the best care. Each case will be decided after careful investigation of all the circumstances including, of course, the ascertainable wishes and feelings of the child, if he or she is old enough to understand what is going on.

As children grow older, the undeniable tilt of the scales in the mother's favour becomes less significant. Yet another factor which will be taken into account, if it is the case, is that the mother may be available on a full-time basis to care for the children whilst the father has a full-time job.

Not every full-time mother succeeds in obtaining a residence order where the father has a full-time job. Again, each case depends on its facts. The guiding principle for the court will always be to discover what will be in the best interests of the child.

Is there a new bias towards fathers?

A fairly recent development has been the media publicity given to cases where fathers have been given residence orders in circumstances where it is the mother who has, in fact, been the breadwinner, possibly because she has better job qualifications, whilst the father has remained at home caring for young children and acting as 'househusband'.

These cases do not, as is often wrongly asserted, demonstrate any change in the approach of the courts to residence disputes. They are merely examples of the court applying the test of what is in the best interests of the children concerned.

Career women may well reflect that they could be shooting themselves in the foot in these days of equality and the 'new man', but it is the parent who represents the significant caring figure on a day-to-day basis in the child's life who is the most likely to obtain a residence order, regardless of whether that parent happens to be mummy or daddy.

Chapter 10: Children – reports to the court

In any case involving children, the judge might ask for the help of one of the children and family reporters, sometimes called family court advisers. This is nothing to be concerned about; it is simply used to assist the court to reach a decision. The court will direct that the report should deal with a specific question or questions, and any report will normally be limited to those questions. However, it occasionally happens that a report will deal with wider matters concerning the child and the various people involved, rather than limiting itself strictly to the areas indicated by the court.

The purpose of such reports is to assist the court by giving a fuller picture of the child's situation and all the factors relevant to the decision the court is asked to make. For example, if there is a dispute over where a child should live, the reporter will visit the child in both homes. If there is a dispute over contact, the reporter may decide to observe the child's reactions to the parent who is asking for contact. However, by ordering a report, the court is not handing over the task of making the decision to the person reporting. The decision is for the court alone.

Nevertheless, it is true to say that the court will almost always pay a great deal of attention to any recommendation made in a report. Indeed, if a judge does not make an order in accordance with a recommendation, he or she must state the reasons for not doing so.

Not every report contains recommendations. Some simply set out the information which the reporter has been able to obtain, possibly together with some impressions of the various people interviewed in the course of the investigation, but making no firm recommendation on what order should be made, leaving it to the court to make the final decision.

The form of the report

Reports may be made in writing or orally. If the matter is not one of urgency, it is usual for the court to request a written report. One reason for this is to give the parties involved in the proceedings some notice of what the reporter will be saying or recommending. This gives people a chance to consider questions that might be put to the officer who prepared the report.

Oral reports

If the matter is very urgent, or if for some other reason the court considers it preferable, the reporter may be requested to give a report verbally.

Case study

Matthew, aged 10, lives with his mother Anne and her new husband James. Residence has been granted to Anne. Sam, Matthew's father, has contact with him for alternate weekends.

One Monday morning Sam goes to court. He asks the judge to discharge the existing residence order and to make an order that Matthew should live with him. He says that when the child had been due to return to his mother on the previous evening, he had broken down in tears and begged Sam to let him stay. Sam says that Matthew was so distressed that he was unable to persuade him to return. Matthew told him that he hated James, and that James was punishing him excessively and unfairly by locking him in a dark cupboard for hours on end.

The judge is faced with an extremely difficult situation. Sam has informed Anne of his application and she too has come to court to ask for an order that Matthew should be returned to her immediately. She categorically denies that James has been punishing Matthew by locking him in an unlit cupboard. She says that Sam is probably making all this up because he wants Matthew to live with him.

It is in this kind of case that a judge might well ask a reporter to talk to Matthew and give oral evidence, rather than wait for a written report which could take weeks or months. It is clearly an urgent matter. Judges are reluctant to change existing orders without good reason. They are even more reluctant to do so on an emergency basis, preferring to wait until all possible evidence, including a report if appropriate, is presented before the court.

On the other hand, if Sam is accurately reporting what has been said by his son, there is obvious cause for concern about whether he should be returned to his mother.

In such an urgent situation, where a judge has asked for an oral report, the period of time allowed might be a few days, or even a few hours. On occasions the reporter might be requested to see both parents and the child in the court building, so that the report can be made immediately.

The reporter would undoubtedly speak to Sam and Anne before attempting to talk to Matthew. He or she would then expect to be introduced to Matthew, preferably by both parents.

The vast majority of reporters are highly skilled and very sensitive in their approach to children. It is extremely unlikely that the reporter would ask Matthew straight away whether he has any problems with his stepfather. It would be usual for the reporter to sit down somewhere quietly with the child, hopefully in a room comfortably furnished for such meetings, and simply have a general chat with him.

Matthew might be asked about his school, what subjects he likes best, which games he prefers, and his friends. Time would be spent encouraging Matthew to relax. Only when his confidence had been gained would the reporter approach the question of what was troubling Matthew, possibly by asking which parent he lived with and how often he saw the other parent.

In this way, the discussion could eventually get to the point where the reporter could raise the question of Matthew's reluctance to return home. It is possible that Matthew has indeed good cause to complain about his stepfather's treatment. On the other hand, it is not unknown for a parent with whom the child is not living to 'manufacture' complaints, by encouraging a child to give a wildly exaggerated account of perfectly normal discipline.

When the reporter is ready, the parents return to court and the oral report is given to the judge. Each parent, or his or her legal representative, will be given an opportunity to put questions to the reporter and to make any submissions as to what the decision about Matthew should be. The judge will then make a decision based on all the evidence that he or she has heard.

Written reports

Matthew's case was one of emergency. Most reports are prepared in writing and at a much more leisurely pace. One of the stated aims of the Children Act was the avoidance of delay in deciding questions relating to children. Judges hearing children's cases are always very keen to decide them as quickly as possible, to avoid causing unnecessary stress to parents and, more importantly, to their children.

In an ideal world, this would mean that delays were kept to a minimum. Unfortunately, although everyone concerned is committed to moving things along as quickly as possible, financial constraints mean that families often have to wait for several months before a case can be heard. The time taken to prepare reports varies from court to court; a period of 14 weeks is normal, but it can be longer. Once the report is available, it may be another few weeks before a contested case can be heard. This means that it is not uncommon for a case to take months to get to court.

When you look at this in human terms, it can result in enormous frustration, even downright misery, for the parents and children involved.

Case study

David and Cheryl have decided to divorce. They have four children: Donna, aged 13, Alan, aged 10, Susannah, aged six and Charlie, aged five. David and Cheryl are unable to agree about who the children should live with after the divorce. Each has applied to the court for a residence order. A report has been ordered.

The family occupy a semi-detached house which is being purchased on mortgage in the joint names of David and Cheryl. It is accepted that whoever obtains the residence order will remain there with the children and the other parent will leave.

Neither of the parents is prepared to leave until the court makes its decision. The house has only three bedrooms, one of them very small. Cheryl is sharing the main bedroom with Susannah. Alan and Charlie share the second bedroom and Donna has the small one. David has a sofa bed in the living room.

David and Cheryl try to behave as normally as possible for the children's sake but the tensions are quite obvious and they are affecting the children. Cheryl does not cook meals for David and she does no washing or ironing for him. She and David barely speak to one another. The whole atmosphere is highly stressful. Donna's schoolwork is suffering. Alan has become cheeky and is getting out of control. Susannah is weepy and clingy, and Charlie, dry at night since he was two, has started bed-wetting again.

Situations like this are depressingly common. Each parent is afraid to leave for fear of losing the 'status quo' argument. 'Status quo' is a Latin expression popular with family lawyers. Roughly translated, it means 'the existing situation'. Lawyers arguing a case will place much emphasis on the benefits to a child of not interfering with the status quo – the situation to which the child is accustomed.

It cannot be denied that family court reporters and judges are reluctant to interfere with the status quo, where it appears to be working reasonably well, on the ground that interference might bring about a worse situation. It follows that if you are the parent with the care of the child when a residence dispute comes to court, you have an undoubted advantage.

So a family lawyer would be unable to advise either David or Cheryl to leave home pending a resolution of their dispute. The parent who left would immediately give the other the advantage.

Far too many families are forced to live under this kind of stress. Unless more resources can be directed towards the provision of an increased number of judges, family court reporters and court buildings, there seems little hope of improving things.

The preparation of the report

The reporting officer has the duty of investigating all those matters to which the court has directed his or her attention, and will probably begin by reading any documentation available on the court file. Sometimes there will be statements by the parents or other witnesses, if these have been ordered by the judge. In other cases the court might direct that no statements should be filed until all parties have had a chance to read the report. Statements can contain hurtful allegations, so the court may delay the filing of such evidence to try to keep the heat out of the situation for as long as possible.

Family reporting officers are, of course, individuals. Each one approaches the task of preparing a report in his or her own way, but there are certain guidelines that they must follow.

Case study

Delia and Kevin have a six-year-old son, Colin. Delia and Kevin are living apart. Both have applied for residence orders. The court has ordered a report directed to the question of whether it would be in Kevin's best interests to live with his mother or his father.

Delia lives in the home she originally shared with Kevin, a two-bedroom flat. No one else lives there. Kevin has moved to another two-bedroom flat, so the accommodation that could be offered to the child by each parent is similar.

The reporting officer interviews Delia, alone and with Colin. Both interviews take place in Delia's flat. The officer then interviews Kevin, alone and with Colin. Both these interviews take place at the offices of social services in the area. The report is eventually filed and makes a firm recommendation that a residence order should be granted to Delia.

There may be many good reasons for that recommendation, but Kevin would have a legitimate reason to challenge it because the court of appeal has made it clear that when a report is ordered on the question of residence, the reporting officer should observe the child with each parent in his or her home environment, unless exceptional circumstances make that impossible.

The child's wishes and feelings

The importance of the child's own wishes and feelings has already been mentioned. In most cases, it will be the reporting officer who will communicate those wishes and feelings to the court.

When arguments about children get as far as the court, adult emotions and tempers are likely to be running at a high level. Parents will convince themselves that their children's wishes and feelings are identical with their own.

The temptation for a parent to encourage the child to tell the reporting officer what that parent wants the officer to hear can be too great. This leads to the desperately sad scenario where a child can be subjected to the most intolerable emotional pressure from one or both parents. The parent becomes so wrapped up in the determination to 'win' that the effects of the emotional temperature on the child are completely disregarded.

In some cases, parents just never give up on the battle, even after the court decision has been made. They go on subjecting their children to pressure, to get back at the other parent. The unfortunate children of such parents often bear the emotional scars into their adult lives, with consequential effects on their own ability to form relationships.

Questioning the reporting officer

The report will normally be filed some time before the hearing date, and copies will be sent to all concerned. At this stage, as at all stages, the parents can, and often do, make their own decision without the need for a court hearing. If there has to be a hearing, it will be possible to question the reporting officer. If you are representing yourself and you wish to ask questions about the report, you must ask the court in advance to ensure that the officer will be available on the day of the hearing.

If you yourself are asking the questions, it is a good idea to make a list of them before coming to court. Always ask questions as politely as you can. The judge will never be impressed by rudeness. You can be sure that the judge will listen with close attention to any questions, and to the replies given, before making a decision.

Chapter 11:
Child support

What is child support maintenance?

Child support maintenance is an amount of money which a non-resident parent pays regularly as a contribution to the financial support of his or her child.

Until April 1993, when the parents of a child had separated the usual means of obtaining a financial contribution towards the maintenance of the child was by way of a court order.

The Child Support Act, which came into force in 1993, completely changed the approach to child maintenance. Unfortunately, the Child Support Agency (CSA), set up under the Act, suffered from the ridiculously complex system of assessment which had been enacted.

The objectives behind the child support legislation were understandable. First, it formed part of an overall determination by the government of the day to emphasise the responsibility of parents for their own children. In 1989, the Children Act had started the process of underlining that responsibility as opposed to the previous importance placed on parental rights.

In 1991, the Criminal Justice Act had extended the powers of the court to impose penalties on those with parental responsibility for delinquent children. The Child Support Act was the third plank in the programme.

Financial considerations were of considerable significance. There had been growing concern about the level of payments being ordered by courts, and the resultant burden on the state when social security payments had to make up the difference between the maintenance ordered and Income Support rates. Throughout the 1980s, attempts made to persuade courts to make orders in line with current Income Support rates had been largely unsuccessful. In 1990, the average maintenance ordered for a child of any age up to 18 was £18 per week. In the same year, the National Foster Care Association was recommending payments of £34.02 per week for a child under the age of five.

Increasing numbers of parents were separating; the consequently increased burden on the taxpayer was becoming insupportable. Having failed to get the courts to raise the level of orders, the Government set up the CSA as a completely separate entity, under government control.

It soon became clear, however, that aspects of the child support scheme were causing considerable public disquiet. At first it was hoped that the difficulties were just teething problems which could be remedied by fine tuning but it became obvious that the trouble was more deep-seated than that.

'Caring' and 'absent'

One of the most tactless aspects of the child support scheme was its use of terminology. It ought to have been foreseeable that to describe parents as either 'caring' or 'absent' was going to cause distress. This should have been particularly obvious in the context of the Children Act, which had just deliberately replaced the emotive 'custody' and 'access' orders by 'residence' and 'contact'.

Not every parent who does not have day-to-day care of his or her child is in that position from choice. Many parents who do not live with their children are still concerned, loving parents, who wish to play as full a part in the lives of their children as possible. It was hardly surprising that such parents found being categorised as 'absent' hurtful, particularly when it was contrasted with 'caring'. Thankfully, the insensitivity of this was appreciated and changes were introduced to describe parents more neutrally as 'resident' and 'non-resident'.

However, it was a bad start and matters were made worse by the rigid and complex formula for the calculation of a parent's liability. The rigidity was intended to ensure that every absent parent had his or her contribution worked out in accordance with a strict mathematical calculation which was applied in every case. This was in contrast with the somewhat haphazard process in operation previously, when two judges hearing different cases in the same court could make two completely different maintenance orders given the same figures to work on. Unfortunately, experience soon demonstrated that assessments by the agency were just as likely to result in unfairness.

The formula did not make allowances for some of the outgoings of the contributing parent, to the point where he or she could be reduced to an income below the Income Support level by its operation. Payment of instalments in relation to certain debts was not taken into account, for example. If the contributing parent lived at some distance from the children, cost of travel to and from contact visits was not taken into account, which was another cause for considerable concern.

Second wives bitterly resented the levels of contribution assessed for the children of their husbands' first marriages, particularly where the first wife had remarried and lived in comfortable financial circumstances with her new husband.

Natural fathers

The parents liable to maintain a child under the child support law are the child's natural parents, or his or her adoptive parents. Before the Child Support Act came into force, a father would have been liable for any child he had treated as a child of the family during the marriage. This change in the law has had some unforeseen consequences.

Case study

When Ben met Sherrie she already had a baby, Rachel, who was a few months old. Ben and Sherrie married and Ben always treated Rachel as his own daughter. Ben and Sherrie had two more children, Marcel and Barnabas. Had Ben and Sherrie separated, Ben would be liable to maintain Marcel and Barnabas under child support law, but not Rachel, even though he had always treated Rachel in exactly the same way as his own sons. This would undoubtedly leave Rachel, if now a teenager, feeling hurt and bewildered that a difference should be made between herself and her brothers, when she had always looked on Ben as her own father too. If Sherrie had to apply for Income Support after the separation, the agency would ask her to name Rachel's father, in order that he could be traced and made to pay maintenance for Rachel.

Naming the father

With the new changes to legislation, a mother on Income Support or Income-Based Jobseeker's Allowance, must name the father of her child. If she refuses, she can be penalised by a reduction in the amount of benefit she is paid, unless she can show that to identify the father would put her or any child living with her at risk.

This has the unfortunate practical result that a father who has used violence against the mother or a child living with her in the past will be able to evade responsibility for child support. In the circumstances, it is hardly surprising that responsible and law-abiding fathers see the operation of the law as unfair.

As only the natural parent is liable to maintain the child, some fathers have tried to deny paternity in order to escape liability. Under the old law, if a child had been accepted as a child of the family by the father, he would have been liable to maintain that child when his marriage broke down.

A few fathers who had suspected that a child was not their own have wished to put that suspicion to proof by means of DNA testing. Applications in such circumstances have serious repercussions so far as the unfortunate child is concerned, not to mention the effect on the relationship of the divorced parents.

Applying for child support

Who can apply?

The agency normally only deals with cases where both parents live in Great Britain or Northern Ireland, although an order could be made in respect of a non-resident parent employed abroad by a company here. You can apply if:

(a) you are a parent of a child or children who are living with you whilst the other parent lives somewhere else, unless you already have a court maintenance or written maintenance agreement made before 5 April 1993;

(b) children who are not your own live with you whilst their parent or parents live somewhere else;

(c) you are the non-resident parent and you wish to have an assessment carried out to show the amount of maintenance you ought to pay.

If a child spends time with both parents, the maintenance assessment can be adjusted to take account of this, depending on how much time the child spends with each.

A non-resident parent can pay the resident parent directly by cheque, standing order or postal order. Alternatively, payments can be made through the agency, weekly, monthly or at some other agreed intervals. If the paying parent fails to make payments and does not have an acceptable excuse for the failure, the payments can be deducted from that parent's wages or salary by his or her employers.

The future for child support

There has been enormous dissatisfaction with the operation of the CSA. Resident parents complained that if the other parent refused to make payment, they could easily get away with not doing so. Non-resident parents complained that assessments were far too high. Taxpayers suspected that enormous sums of public money were being wasted to bolster up a system which was inefficient, penalised the poorest members of society and seemed to enable many high-earning non-resident parents to escape making appropriate payments. In July 1998, figures were disclosed revealing that one-third of the receipts from non-resident parents and almost four out of five maintenance balances for full assessments were for the wrong amount! Proposals for reform were published at that time, but reform was delayed until March 2003.

The new scheme is designed to be more transparent and easier for parents to understand. It is hoped that the agency will be able to spend more time enforcing payments and ensuring that children get appropriate support. It is based on a simple percentage rate – 15 per cent of net income for one child, 20 per cent for two children and 25 per cent for three children or more.

Non-resident parents with net incomes of less than £100 a week, or those receiving a wide range of benefits, will only have to pay a flat rate of £5 a week. A new child maintenance premium will mean that, for the first time, resident parents on Income Support or Income-Based Jobseeker's Allowance will be able to keep up to £10 a week of any maintenance paid for the children.

Initially, the new scheme was introduced for new cases only. Existing cases will be reassessed when the Government is confident that it is seen to be working well.

Where the non-resident parent lives in a household with other children, the net earned income can be reduced for calculation purposes. If you think that this may apply to you, the CSA will be able to advise you. The discount for shared care ('staying contact') is now more generous. Again, it depends on how many nights a year your child stays with you. The CSA can do the calculation for you.

Chapter 12:
Child abuse

Divorce is always traumatic, but never more so than when one parent suspects that the other may be a child abuser. The most horrifying crimes committed in our society today are those against children. Our revulsion against these crimes is intensified because children are, by definition, innocent and defenceless. The younger the child, the more he or she ought to be entitled to protection and love from adults. Children are naturally trusting and affectionate. Betrayal of that trust is one of the hardest things in the world to forgive.

In recent years, people seem to assume that child abuse is limited to sexual abuse, which is hardly surprising in view of the publicity that this form of abuse has received in the media. Yet abuse can take other forms: it can be physical. Appalling cases of cruelty, like the torture of eight-year-old Victoria Climbié, stir up public compassion and incomprehension and the story is distressingly familiar. The public enquiry into Victoria's death has resulted in governmental plans to set up ministerial supervision of the operation of agencies concerned with the protection of children. Whether the rather cumbersome and bureaucratic set-up suggested is going to make any difference has yet to be seen. Many professionals would have preferred to see the appointment of a Children's Ombudsman, independent of the Government, to be a champion and watchdog for children's interests.

Neglect is another common form of abuse. The 'home alone' cases, regularly reported in the media, are raising awareness of this. Cases of neglect do appear to occur more frequently than in the past. This may be due, as with other forms of abuse, to the fact that increasing numbers of children are living in households where one of the parental figures, particularly the father, is not the natural parent. It may be partially due to economic deprivation or unemployment, factors which induce feelings of depression and hopelessness, coupled with a lack of ability to cope with the demands of bringing up a family. It could be due to sheer ignorance of what the basic minimum needs of a child are.

Emotional abuse is more subtle, but it can be as damaging to a child as physical abuse. We will return to this topic later in the chapter.

We warn our children against strangers. We like to comfort ourselves with the belief that only strangers can be a danger. Unfortunately, this is far from the truth. Many more children are abused by members of their own family or people who are familiar to them than by strangers. Sadly, it is important to be on the alert for signs of abuse, even among children we know.

Sexual abuse

Children are sexually abused at all ages, even as babies. Abuse can happen to any child, boy or girl, rich or poor; the abuser can be male or female. Is sexual abuse of children more common now than in the past? Or is it that we are becoming more aware and vigilant, so that more instances are coming to light?

Alternatively, is it due to more help being available and more victims being prepared to speak up? Has the proliferation of pornographic material relating to children in recent years had an effect on the unstable personalities of potential abusers? Does the publicity given to child abuse in the media have the effect of encouraging further abuse?

Experts debate these questions interminably; no doubt they will continue to do so. What is certain is that even 20 years ago, court cases in which allegations of sexual abuse were involved were comparatively rare; now they are depressingly common.

False allegations

Since the problem of sexual abuse of children came so prominently to public attention, there has been an extremely worrying development. In some cases, where there is a high level of parental conflict and the resident parent wishes to terminate contact between a child and the other parent, an allegation will be made that the other is sexually abusing the child. It is particularly easy to make such an allegation in the case of a very young child. The parent making the allegation, usually the mother, almost invariably achieves his or her aim in that contact with the other parent is stopped, or is only permitted under the supervision of some other adult.

Most local authorities, hard pressed by financial restraints and the current difficulties in recruitment of social work staff, are neither willing nor able to provide such supervision for regular contact. The parent making the allegation will object to every supervisor suggested by the other parent, so that eventually the other parent will be faced with the choice of paying for supervision by an independent social worker or being deprived of further contact.

Needless to say, the damage done to a child by a false allegation can be incalculable. First, there is the loss of the relationship with the falsely accused parent. Even if the allegation is eventually found to have been false, months will have passed whilst it was being investigated.

During that time any contact between parent and child will have taken place in the totally artificial environment of supervision. Investigations will be going on. The child will be interviewed by police officers and social workers, perhaps on more than one occasion. An intimate medical examination, extremely distressing to the child, may take place. There may be more than one physical examination. A psychiatrist or child psychologist may be invited to report. It is not unusual for a young child to have to undergo several sessions with such experts.

It has to be said that the quality and expertise of the various professionals who interview children in these situations can vary tremendously. The skilled experts are sensitive and objective. They do not approach the interviews with their minds already made up as to the truth of the allegations. They do not call interviews 'disclosure' sessions, implying that they expect confirmation of already formed opinions. They do not ask the child questions which suggest the answers that will fit in with their preconceptions.

Unfortunately for many children and many parents, there are professionals who fall far short of this standard. These are the police officers, social workers, doctors and child psychiatrists who accept without question allegations made by parents in situations where, with minimal investigation, it would be possible to discern the residual bitterness from a broken relationship which should automatically put professionals on their guard.

The type of question asked by professionals overkeen to obtain 'disclosure' is that of the social worker who produced an anatomically explicit male doll to a four-year-old. Helping the child to undress the doll, the social worker prompted, 'He looks a little bit like Daddy, doesn't he?' The child examined the doll thoughtfully, then said, 'Not really. My Daddy's got a moustache.'

The American experience

In America, false allegations made in the context of divorce have become so common that the syndrome is abbreviated to SAID (sexual allegations in divorce). Allegations made in the context of an acrimonious separation are now treated with great reserve in the United States but the tragedy for some children and their falsely accused parents is that it has taken some years for lawyers and other professionals to appreciate the danger of accepting allegations in this context.

Not only does the child lose a parent, he or she also has to grow up in the care of a parent who promotes the belief that sexual abuse did take place, with all the resultant consequences to emotional stability in adolescence and adulthood which that belief entails. Parents who deliberately inflict that burden on their own children for their own selfish ends must bear a responsibility quite as heavy as that of a parent who has actually sexually abused a child.

Parents who make false allegations may not always be fully aware of what they are doing. A mother who would really like to cut the father out of the child's life may misinterpret some perfectly innocent remark made by the child. She reports her suspicions to social services. Much will depend upon who speaks to the child. An over-zealous social worker, with little real knowledge of sexually abused children, can do irreparable harm by approaching the child in the wrong way. The social worker confirms the mother's suspicion. The mother, secretly delighted, convinces herself that it isn't she who is curtailing the father's contact, but social services.

Young children are suggestible by nature. They quickly learn, without understanding what they are being asked, that certain responses to questions from professionals are more welcome than others.

An assertion frequently made is that a young child always tells the truth, so children must always be believed. This ignores the inconvenient fact, known to any parent, that young children have vivid imaginations. They may be telling the truth in the sense that they believe what they say. But that does not necessarily mean that what they are saying is true.

An American researcher came up with disturbing conclusions. One of his experiments was with a group of five-year-olds in a classroom. He told the children that a man would be coming into the classroom and that this man would behave badly. Shortly afterwards, a man came in. He stayed for a few minutes, did nothing and did not speak. Afterwards the children were asked to describe what he did.

Some of the children reported accurately that the man did nothing. But several of them recounted naughty things he had done in great detail. Because it had been suggested to them that he would behave badly, they supplied details of his bad behaviour through their own imaginations. It is important to realise that they were not lying. They believed what they said.

An even more surprising result came from a second experiment. A group of young children were interviewed individually. Each was asked if she or he had ever had a finger caught in a mousetrap. Each said that this had never happened.

On several subsequent days each child was asked the same question in a neutral manner. No suggestive questioning was used. They were simply asked again whether they had ever had a finger caught in a mousetrap. Some of the children began to say that it had happened and to supply details about the occasion.

One little boy constructed an elaborate account of a time when he and his brother had been playing in the cellar of the family home whilst their father was chopping wood. His brother, he said, had pushed him and he had fallen into a pile of chopped wood. A mousetrap, concealed in the wood pile, had caught his finger. He had been taken by ambulance to the hospital. His mother, father and brother had visited him in hospital.

The father of this child was asked to explain to him that he had imagined all this. The child listened to his father, but next time he was interviewed he recounted the same details and insisted that all this had really happened. Clearly, he believed that it had and so he was speaking the truth.

These experiments cast considerable doubt on the doctrine that children must invariably be believed. If you substitute for the neutral questioning in the experiment, the emotionally loaded questioning by a much loved parent who, consciously or unconsciously, wants to believe that abuse has occurred, it seems all too possible that a child can become convinced that abuse has taken place when it has not.

This means that professionals should be particularly careful about making a diagnosis of abuse based solely on what a young child may be saying in the absence of other evidence. They should be especially on their guard when there is an acrimonious relationship between the child's parents.

Emotional abuse

The making of a false allegation that a child has been sexually abused is one form of emotional abuse of a child. Emotional abuse may not, of course, be as easy to detect as physical or sexual abuse, but it can certainly be as damaging to a child.

It is well known that sexual abusers also exert emotional abuse over their victims. Almost invariably the sexual abuse will be accompanied by threats of what will happen to the child if the abuse is disclosed. These can range from threats that the child will be called a liar, to threats of violence, even murder. When the abuser is a family member the child may be threatened that he or she will be taken into care and will not be allowed to live at home ever again, or that he or she will be responsible for breaking up the family.

Children abused by a parent often retain feelings of love for that parent. They are placed in an intolerable situation. They may not want to get the abusing parent into trouble. They may not even be aware that they are being abused. Many abused children, particularly young children, simply assume that what is happening to them happens to all children.

Above all, the abused child may desperately want to stay at home. He or she wants the abuse to stop but the threat of being taken into care may prevent any disclosure. Lawyers are all too familiar with cases where children who have disclosed abuse, and been taken into care, will withdraw the disclosures simply because they want to go home.

In cases of parental abuse, if the parent is prepared to acknowledge it, apologise to the child and undergo therapy, it is possible that they may be reunited. However, this will usually mean a period of months spent in family therapy to ensure that the child will be fully protected and feel safe before the parent can return home.

Children as weapons

Children can be emotionally abused in situations where there is no form of physical abuse. Parents with care who persistently make difficulties about a child having contact with the other parent are emotionally abusing their children, whether they realise it or not.

Similarly, it is emotional abuse of a child for one parent to denigrate the other to the child. Most parents who allow themselves to criticise the child's other parent would be horrified to be told that they are abusing the child but they are undoubtedly doing just that.

The vital thing for parents to remember is that relationships may founder, but parenthood lasts for life. If they can only make themselves behave civilly towards one another for the sake of their children, the benefits to the children will be huge and they may even learn to like one another again.

What if you suspect a child is being abused?

Most of us have a natural reluctance to interfere in other people's lives but children do need the protection of adults. If you have reason to believe that a child is being abused in some way, you should contact the social services department of your local authority. Social workers will check the situation. You need not worry that your name will be disclosed.

Signs that a child is being abused

Schoolteachers, doctors or social workers sometimes notice that a child is behaving in a way which makes them suspicious of abuse. Abused children may act in sexually precocious ways with other children or with adults. They can become withdrawn and tearful. They can exhibit fear of adults. There can be physical signs, such as otherwise unexplained soreness.

Abused children often have nightmares. Someone who knows the child well, a family member, close friend of the family or teacher, may notice that the child's behaviour has changed in a worrying way, when there is no apparent reason for the change.

If there is a court case will the child have to give evidence?

When a child has been sexually abused and the abuser is charged with a criminal offence, the child sometimes has to give evidence. It has been recognised how traumatic an experience this can be for any child. Arrangements are now usually made for the child to give evidence in a room away from the court, by video link, in the presence of some reassuring adult, such as the child protection officer dealing with the case with whom the child will already be familiar.

In a civil case, the child never has to give evidence. An interview with the child by a police officer, social worker or psychiatrist, designed to get the child to disclose details of the abuse, should be recorded on video, although it has to be said that this is not the invariable practice. If a video has been made it can be used in the court proceedings.

For whatever reason, sexual abuse of children appears to have become more widespread. Perhaps the only good outcome is that facilities for helping victims of abuse through counselling and other therapy are now widely available.

Children will only be safe if everyone takes responsibility for protecting them. We must all be prepared to report any concerns to the authorities.

Chapter 13:
Domestic violence

We seem to live in an increasingly violent society. We constantly see and hear reports of horrific violence suffered by women at the hands of men, appalling violence inflicted on children by adults, mindless violence against elderly people and the mentally or physically disabled, racial violence, even violence committed in the name of religion.

There are those who are not convinced that the level of violence has actually increased. They argue that because violence is given more prominence in the media today, we are given the impression that the problem is a new one. They point to the Victorian society depicted by Charles Dickens and to criminals like the nefarious Jack the Ripper.

Others think that the media have to bear a heavy responsibility for today's levels of violence. It would be difficult, if not impossible, to spend an evening watching television without having to view at least one scene of explicit violence. The producers of news bulletins no longer shrink from depicting the horrors of war or terrorism in the starkest possible detail. Fictional programme producers seem to believe that viewers are attracted by similarly explicit scenes.

The wide availability of pornographic material on the Internet, much of it involving violence, is another factor contributing to an acceptance of and desire for more violence in daily life. Huge sums of money are spent on advertising by publicists convinced that it will encourage people to buy their products but it is denied that media promotion of violence can have any effect.

The judge who tried the two young boys convicted of the murder of the toddler Jamie Bulger is reported to have expressed concern about the possibility that those children had been copying what they had seen on video film. The debate will probably never be resolved but one thing is quite certain: there is a high level of violence in our society and much of that violence takes place in the home.

Battered women

Many people imagine that the sort of man who inflicts violence on his wife is likely to be an uneducated lout. Unfortunately, this stereotype is very misleading. Professional and educated men are capable of violence against women, men who would be considered perfect gentlemen by friends and business colleagues.

The women victims are often reluctant to seek help or to tell anyone else about what is happening. A bruised eye will be explained as the result of an accident with an open cupboard door. A limp resulting from a kick will have been caused by a fall downstairs. GPs and casualty units are all too familiar with such lame stories.

Shocked outsiders will ask why a wife subjected to violence doesn't just leave, or do something else about it. Many victims truly believe that the man will change. He has apologised, told her that he didn't understand what came over him, promised it will never happen again. She wants to believe that, she may still love him, so she hides the problem. Research has shown that most victims have been hit more than 50 times before they report it to police; even then they are often unwilling to instigate criminal proceedings.

Victims may also blame themselves. Husbands tell them that it is their fault, that they have asked for it. Even though they should know how untrue that is, they come to believe it. Shame and pride induce them to cover the violence up. It is such a humiliating experience that they lose their confidence and their respect for themselves. Frequently, the abusing man will tell the woman that no one will believe her, and she almost comes to accept that.

Children who have lived with violence between parental figures in the home often grow into adulthood to repeat the pattern. The first few years of life are vitally important in the development of our future personalities. Our direct experiences inevitably shape out adult attitudes and behaviour.

The sons of wife beaters often develop their own relationships in the same pattern. Violence has been imprinted in their subconscious as a integral part of what it means for a man and woman to relate to one another.

This can also be true of their victims. A 17-year-old girl was giving evidence in court about her relationship with an older man who habitually beat her. She was an attractive and obviously intelligent young girl. The judge asked her why she had put up with the violence and she seemed almost surprised by the question. 'When I was little,' she said 'my Dad always used to hit my Mum. So when my boyfriend hits me I know he loves me.'

Domestic violence is not only perpetrated by men against women. There can be few lawyers practising family law who have not encountered cases where women have made a habit of assaulting their husbands or boyfriends.

It is even more humiliating for a man to have to admit that he is the victim of violence at the hands of a woman. These cases are relatively uncommon, principally because the man is usually more powerful and physically stronger, so he can defend himself. Also, a man abused in this way will be even more ashamed and unlikely to want to admit it.

The changing attitude of the police

Not so long ago the majority of police officers would have been dismissive of any incidents where domestic violence was involved. Injuries serious enough to warrant a criminal prosecution had they been inflicted between strangers would be disregarded if inflicted by a husband on his wife. This attitude had more than a little to do with the view of the law that a wife was the possession of her husband, to do with as he pleased.

It is only comparatively recently that the courts have accepted that it is possible for a woman to be raped by her husband. For hundreds of years the approach of the law was that a husband had an absolute right to sexual intercourse with his wife whenever he wanted it and whatever her feelings about it.

It is now accepted by the police that domestic violence is a crime. Nobody has the right to assault you physically, sexually or emotionally. Victims who get in touch with the police find them to be committed to dealing with them sympathetically and offering practical help and advice. Most police stations now have community safety units where men and women officers, who have received special training, are able to give assistance and advice; officers can also enlist the help of other agencies, social services and housing departments, for example. All police officers have instructions to treat domestic assaults as criminal offences and to prosecute the offenders if appropriate.

Aims of domestic violence units

Police community safety units were set up with the following objectives:

(a) To provide a readily accessible service to victims and to assist them in making reasoned choices.

(b) To help co-ordinate social, voluntary and caring agencies, to pool ideas and to ensure consistency of approach in dealing with domestic violence.

(c) To raise the level of consciousness of police officers and of the public to the lonely and vulnerable plight of women subjected to violence in the home.

(d) To provide a professional strategic approach to any investigation.

How can the police help?

First, a victim will be given the moral support of having someone who will listen sympathetically. A medical examination can be arranged if necessary. The victim will then be advised about the various options open to him or her.

If the police are satisfied that a crime has been committed, the abuser can be charged and tried in a criminal court, but domestic violence can also be dealt with under the civil law without charging the abuser with a criminal offence.

(a) Criminal proceedings

The victim will have any criminal proceedings explained to him or her. If necessary, a police officer from the unit might attend court with the victim to give moral support. The officer would also keep the victim informed about what is happening with regard to the court proceedings. For example, bail conditions might be imposed on a man who has assaulted his wife pending a full court hearing. Very often those conditions would include a ban on his return home, for the protection of the wife. If the victim does not wish to take the matter to the criminal court, the domestic violence unit will keep a record of what has happened, together with photographs and any other evidence. If there should be a further assault and the victim then decides to take the matter to the criminal court, the records can help to show that there has been a pattern of violence.

(b) Civil law

Police officers can refer victims to local solicitors who specialise in dealing with domestic violence in the civil courts. A new law makes it a crime to breach a civil injunction, giving the police the power to arrest the culprit immediately, without the necessity for a further court order.

Non-molestation orders

A non-molestation order is made by the court to prevent your partner from using violence against you or from threatening you with violence, or from intimidating, harassing or pestering you. If that order is disobeyed by your partner, he or she could be sent to prison. In some cases the court will not actually make an order but will accept an undertaking instead. An undertaking is a solemn promise made to the court and has exactly the same effect as an order, in that a breach of an undertaking may result in the person being sent to prison. This will always be explained very carefully by the judge to the person giving the undertaking.

Case study

Marie has been assaulted by her husband Reg. She asks the County court for an order protecting her from further violence. Reg denies that he has assaulted Marie. The judge does not need to hear evidence from either Marie or Reg. The case is dealt with by the judge asking Reg if he is willing, without admitting that he has assaulted Marie in the past, to promise that he will not do so in the future. Reg agrees to do this, as it is pointed out to him that no finding is being made against him and he is making no admission of guilt. The judge then explains to Reg that his promise to the court will be in the form of an undertaking, which Reg has to sign. Reg's undertaking is that he will not 'use or threaten to use violence against Marie'. The judge will explain very carefully to Reg that if he breaks that promise he risks being sent to prison.

In many cases, the experience of appearing before a court and having to give such a promise has the effect of making a husband realise for the first time how shameful his behaviour has been.

Case study

Lou has been beaten up by her husband Max. She goes to the County court to get protection. Max denies that he has assaulted Lou and claims that the injuries she suffered were the result of a fall on the stairs. Max refuses to give undertakings and wants a full hearing by the court. Both Lou and Max give evidence and the judge accepts Lou's evidence. The judge can then make various different orders, according to the gravity of the assault and the other circumstances of the case. One order which will certainly be made is that Max should not use or threaten to use violence against Lou.

If you have children and there has been any violence or threat of violence to them, the court can include the children in the protection order. The order can cover any other matters which may be important in any particular case; for example, your husband could be forbidden to telephone you or to loiter outside your place of work or the children's school.

Occupation orders

The courts also have the power to decide who should occupy your family home. If there has been serious violence and you do not feel that it is safe to continue living with your husband or wife, or if you have actually left home because of the violence and do not wish to return whilst he or she is still living there, you may want to apply for an occupation order. This would be an order that he or she leaves the home so that you can occupy it.

Ordering someone to leave their home is clearly a very serious matter; occupation orders are only granted when the court takes the view that the situation cannot be dealt with by non-molestation undertakings or orders.

Who can apply for an occupation order?

You can apply for an occupation order if:

(a) you are the sole or joint tenant of your home, or married to someone who is;

(b) you are the owner or co-owner of your home, or married to someone who is;

(c) you have been married to the person who has a legal right to occupy the property;

(d) you have lived as man and wife with the person who has a legal right to occupy the property.

Occupation orders can be granted for six months. In certain circumstances the period can be extended.

What you can do in an emergency

In any emergency you can contact the police by dialling 999. Women's Aid have a national helpline (see Appendix for the contact details) which offers support, help and information to women who are experiencing, or who have experienced, domestic violence. If you need somewhere to stay or you need advice about legal matters, you will be able to talk to a volunteer in confidence. Even if all you need is someone to talk to, you can talk for as long as you need and as often as you like.

Women's Aid also have about 250 refuges in the UK. These are safe houses which offer temporary accommodation for women and children who need to escape from domestic violence. The addresses and telephone numbers of refuges are secret, which makes it difficult for abusers to track their victims down. You can stay for a few days, giving you time to think and make plans, or you might stay for several months. Women's Aid workers will help you find accommodation if you need it.

If you are a victim of violence

Please remember, if you are a victim:

(a) you are not alone; there are people who are willing to help;

(b) you are not to blame; the abuser is the one with the problem;

(c) contact the police; they will advise you of your options;

(d) the police will let you make your own decisions;

(e) the police will respect your confidentiality.

Chapter 14:
Child abduction

'Please, please, get my baby back for me!' How many times have you heard that desperate plea and seen the tear-streaked face of some frantic mother on a television newscast or newspaper front page?

Then there will be the photograph of the child who has been snatched by his or her estranged father or mother. These occurrences are always times of enormous stress, not only for the parent from whom the child has been snatched but also, and even more importantly, for the unfortunate child concerned.

Kidnapping, at one time, was a crime almost invariably committed by people who were strangers to the child, motivated by an intention to blackmail the parents of the victim into paying huge sums of money for the child's return. It happened more frequently in the United States; the kidnapped child would often come from a very wealthy family.

The type of child-snatching we are all too familiar with nowadays is quite different. It usually occurs when parents have separated on acrimonious terms and one parent (usually the father) does not accept that their child should live with the other. As family breakdown has become more common worldwide, international kidnapping – or child abduction as it is called legally – happens more and more often.

Case study

Mervyn and Dee have divorced. They disagreed about who their seven-year-old twin daughters, Lara and Emma, should live with. There was a court battle lasting three days, during which hurtful allegations were made on both sides. The court made a residence order in favour of Dee. Mervyn is a wealthy man. He likes his own way and is used to getting it. He has kept the twins' passports. One day he simply turns up at their school, tells the teacher that Dee has agreed that he collect the girls, drives them to the airport and flies with them to a country which has no reciprocal arrangements with England about the enforcement of orders relating to children.

> *The court here orders Mervyn to return the twins to Dee. He ignores the order. Dee is naturally extremely distressed but Mervyn has forgotten one important fact. He still has a home, a business and bank accounts in this country. In a case like this, the court can and will make an order that unless Mervyn obeys the order to return the children, his assets will be confiscated. Mervyn cannot afford to lose the assets he has here, so he brings the twins back. On his return, he is arrested and brought before the court. He has flouted the court order and so is in contempt of court. He can be sent to prison for this offence.*

In some cases a child may be wrongfully removed by one parent from the care of the other when both parents are still in this country. Any order made by the court will be easier to enforce if the children have not been taken abroad. However, it can happen that the parent applying for the return of the child does not know where the other parent has taken the child. In those circumstances, the court can make a 'seek and find' order instructing an officer of the court (called a 'tipstaff') to make enquiries and trace the child.

The court may give leave for details about the child to be published in the media. This is exceptional, because the general rule is that no details about a child concerned in any court case may be published. Only when other means have failed will leave be given for descriptions and photographs of the missing child and the abducting parent to be published, in the hope that these may jog the memory of some member of the public, enabling the child to be traced.

The court can also order anyone who might be able to give some information about the whereabouts of a missing child to come to court to be asked about what they know. Grandparents, other relatives or close friends of the kidnapper, who might possibly have information about the address to which the child has been taken, may have to attend court.

If you believe your child has been abducted

If your child has been snatched and you believe that there is a real risk that the other parent may be planning to take the child out of the country, the police should be told immediately. If the child is under the age of 16, you do not have to have a court order forbidding his or her removal before contacting the police. The police will contact immigration officers and warn them to keep watch for the child and the parent at seaports and airports. If the child is 16 or 17 years old, you need a court order before the police can act. If the case is really urgent, the court can make an order on the day you apply for it.

Before the police act, they must be satisfied that the danger that the child will be taken out of the country is real and imminent.

It is important that you get legal advice as soon as possible. Solicitors are very busy people, but if you explain the situation over the telephone a solicitor will normally see you very quickly.

Passports

You can write to your regional office of the United Kingdom Passport Agency asking the agency not to issue a passport for your child on the application of the other parent. The agency will usually need to see some court order which has been made about the child, but you do not normally have to have an order if you are an unmarried mother. If you believe that an application may already have been made, or is soon to be made, you can telephone the agency.

If the other parent is not a British national, he or she may try to obtain a passport for the child from his or her own embassy, high commission or consulate in this country. You or your solicitor could write to request the officials of that embassy, high commission or consulate not to issue such a passport. They are not obliged to do what you ask, but they might do so voluntarily.

When a child has been wrongfully taken abroad

Sadly, it often happens that a child may have been spirited out of the country before anything can be done. With increased speed and ease of travel between one country and another, problems of child abduction became so common that the situation had to be tackled on an international basis. Two international conventions provide for the return of children wrongfully removed from the country where they usually live and taken to another state which recognises one of these conventions. Signatories include the United States, Australia, Canada, New Zealand and most European countries.

Case study

Corinne and Des have been having problems in their marriage. They married in this country and their daughter Belle was born here. Corinne herself is Australian and all her family still live there. Corinne decides to take Belle to Australia. She knows that Des would never agree so, without telling him, she books tickets and flies off with Belle to join her family.

Corinne should not have taken Belle to Australia without the agreement of Des, or an order of the court. Des can obtain a court order here that Corinne bring Belle back. The court in Australia will enforce that order.

Incidentally, Corinne has behaved rather foolishly. A mother who is genuinely feeling lonely and isolated because her marriage has broken down and her family are living far away can apply to the court for permission to take her child or children to live with her near her family, even when the children have been born and brought up here and their father is English.

The court will then make a full enquiry as to whether or not it would be in the best interests of the children to go with the mother or not. It is not unusual for the court to give a mother – or indeed a father – permission to take the children to live abroad in such a case.

Again, it must be emphasised that every case turns on its own facts. There have been cases where such applications have been refused because the court considered that it would be against the interests of the children to have their contact with the parent in England cut off, or limited by geographical distance. Corinne would certainly have prejudiced her chances of obtaining court permission to remove Belle permanently due to her behaviour in taking Belle to Australia without the permission of her father.

It is to be hoped that eventually these conventions will be recognised throughout the world. Tragically, when a child is removed to a country where neither convention is recognised, the courts here are powerless unless, like Mervyn, the snatching parent has assets in this country.

If the child is taken to a convention country

A list of all the countries which belong to one or both of the conventions dealing with child abduction can be obtained from the Child Abduction Unit of the Lord Chancellor's Department (see Appendix for the address). If the child has been taken to one of those countries, staff at the unit will take brief details over the telephone and will send you a questionnaire to complete. When you send back the completed questionnaire you must send with it:

(a) copies of any court orders about the child which clearly show the court seal;

(b) photographs of the child and the person who has taken the child;

(c) any other relevant information which might explain the circumstances of the removal or retention of the child or which may help in locating the child.

The Child Abduction Unit then makes a formal application for the return of the child, arranging for the details supplied on the completed questionnaire to be translated, if necessary. The formal application is sent, by airmail if appropriate, to the central authority of the country to which the child has been taken. The unit will do all it can to speed up matters as far as humanly possible but obviously much depends on the speed with which the other country deals with the case.

Under the conventions, no payment for legal proceedings in the country to which the child has been taken is normally required, although there are exceptions to this, particularly if the country concerned does not operate any publicly funded system, as is the case, for example, with the United States. The Child Abduction Unit will supply information about likely costs, if any.

If the child is taken to a non-convention country

If your child is taken to a country which has not signed one of the conventions, the situation is very much more complicated. If you cannot reach an amicable agreement with the other parent, or whoever has taken the child, you might have to instruct a lawyer in the country to which the child has been taken and institute legal proceedings in that country. The consular department of the Foreign and Commonwealth Office can provide a list of lawyers in any particular country who can correspond in English. Unfortunately, British consular officers in foreign countries cannot give legal advice or act as your legal representative.

Legal proceedings abroad may be costly; public funding here is not available for proceedings outside the country. It may be possible to get public funding assistance from the country where the child has been taken; any lawyer in that country should be able to advise you about this.

Another vitally important consideration is that foreign courts obviously apply their own laws. You might have a very good case in England, but the other parent might have the law on his or her side in the country to which the child has been abducted.

In some countries a mother does not have the same rights over a child as the father. Additionally, if you do not have the same social, cultural or religious background, and it is your intention to bring the child back with you, these factors could well count against you in a foreign court. A lawyer from the country concerned will be able to advise you about all these matters.

How can the Foreign and Commonwealth Office help?

British consuls can:

- provide a list of local lawyers who correspond in English;

- approach local authorities for help in tracing the child;

- with the consent of the other parent, obtain a report on the child;

- draw to the attention of the local authorities the existence of any UK court order (with the UK court's permission);

- help establish and keep open lines of communication;

- provide informal practical help locally.

No consular fees will be charged.

British consuls cannot:

- recover children for parents;

- become involved in illegal attempts to return children;

- pay legal costs;

- fund air travel for parents;

- obtain visas on behalf of parents for the country concerned.

If your child has been abducted within the United Kingdom

Scotland and Northern Ireland have their own legal systems which are different from England and Wales. At one time these differences meant that a person with an English court order for custody, for example, might be faced with the situation where the other parent took the child off to Scotland and obtained a custody order there. The English order might not have been enforceable in Scotland and equally the Scottish order might not have been enforceable in England.

The Family Law Act of 1986 put an end to these problems by providing that the courts for the part of the UK with which the child has the closest long-term connection are the courts where orders may be made about that child. Such orders will be enforced throughout the UK.

To enforce an order in your favour, you must apply to the court which made the order to register it in the court in which you wish to enforce it. Similar arrangements exist between the UK and the Isle of Man.

The government departments and organisations listed at the end of this chapter are used for requests for urgent help or advice. You should not hesitate to contact them if your child has been abducted or if you believe there is a real risk of abduction.

Checklist

If your child has been abducted or you are afraid that abduction may be a possibility in the future, it would be useful to have as much of the following information as possible:

On the child

- Full name

- Date and place of birth

- Passport number, date and place of issue

- Physical description

On the person who has taken or might take the child

- Full name (and any aliases/mother's maiden name if applicable)

- Date and place of birth

- Passport number, date and place of issue

- Occupation

- Probable date of departure

- Departure information (e.g. flight, train, ferry)

- Details of ties to a foreign country, such as names, addresses, etc.

- Telephone numbers of relatives, friends and business contacts

Copies of documents

- Any agreements or court orders which relate to the child

- The child's birth certificate

- Photographs of the child

- Photographs of the person who has removed/retained the child

- Name and address of your solicitor if you have one

You should get advice from a solicitor as soon as possible. You can apply for an order prohibiting the other parent from removing the child from the country. Although the existence of an order does not guarantee that the other parent will not abduct the child, it makes your position stronger in the event that an abduction does take place.

You should also warn the child's school and make sure staff are clear about who can collect the child from school.

Criminal offences

It is a criminal offence for a person connected with a child to take or to send a child under the age of 16 out of the UK without the 'appropriate consent'. A person connected with a child might be a parent, a guardian or someone who has a residence order in respect of the child. If the child's parents were not married to one another at the date of the child's birth, a man who is reasonably believed to be the father is a person connected with the child.

However, if you have a residence order, you are allowed to remove the child or children from the UK for any period of less than one month; you do not have to obtain the consent of anyone else to do so. This is just to ensure that a parent who has a residence order can take the child or children abroad for ordinary holidays without a lot of fuss.

'Appropriate consent' can be given by the child's parents (if the father has parental responsibility) by the guardian if there is one, or any person with a residence or custody order.

It is also a criminal offence, of course, for any other person, who is not connected with the child, to abduct the child.

Child abduction is a complicated area of the law. If at all possible it is best to consult a solicitor if you have a problem connected with a child who has been taken abroad, or who may have been taken abroad wrongfully.

Other sources of information and help

Reunite, the national council for abducted children, provides the following services (see Appendix for the address):

- National advice line
- Child abduction prevention packs
- Newsletters
- Emotional support for parents and families by trained personnel
- Contact with the Parent Support Network
- Continues to develop a national and international lawyers network
- Researches laws of the countries to which children are abducted

Other information and assistance can be provided by your local Citizens Advice Bureau and/or your local police station (telephone numbers can be found in your local directory).

Child Abduction (a free booklet) is available from The Child Abduction Unit, The Foreign and Commonwealth Office, The United Kingdom Passport Office and Reunite (see Appendix for addresses).

Chapter 15:
Eight steps to divorce

If you and your spouse can agree on the important issues of children and the division of property, yours is an uncontested divorce, which means it requires numerous filling out of forms but few or no court appearances. If you refer to the completed forms in this Guide, obtaining your own divorce is not a complicated procedure. Just follow these seven steps:

Step 1. Find your marriage certificate

You will have to file a certified copy of your marriage certificate at court when you start your divorce petition. If yours has been lost, you can obtain a certified copy of it for a fee. You can apply online, by telephone, email, fax or post, with the fee (standard and fast service available) to:

> General Register Office
> PO Box 2
> Southport PR8 2JD
> Tel: 0870 243 7788
> Email: certificate.services@ons.gov.uk
> Website: www.gro.gov.uk

You will need to provide:

- Your full name

- Your spouse's full name

- The date and place of your marriage

If you were married outside England or Wales and do not have your marriage certificate, it will be necessary to get a certified copy from the country where you were married.

Step 2. Start your divorce petition

You can start your divorce by filing your divorce petition with the Principal Registry of the Family Division based at the following address:

First Avenue House
42-49 High Holborn
London WC1V 6NP

Tel: 020 7947 6000

You can also file a divorce petition at any County court, but choose a court near where you live; you may need to make several visits to court before the divorce is completed. Addresses and telephone numbers of divorce County courts can be found in the telephone directory or online at www.courtservice.gov.uk.

The Principal Registry is open Monday to Friday, 10 am to 4:30 pm. The divorce County courts are open Monday to Friday, 10 am to 4 pm.

Court fees

The current fee for filing your divorce petition is £180, although fees are subject to periodic change. The divorce County court staff can confirm the current fees. You can pay the fee in cash, by postal order or by cheque payable to 'H.M. Paymaster General'. There are nominal additional fees for orders for financial support and for records showing you are divorced.

You will not be required to pay the filing fee if you receive:

- Income Support;

- Income-Based Jobseeker's Allowance;

- Working Families' Tax Credit;

- Disabled Person's Tax Credit;

- legal help from a solicitor under the Community Legal Service Fund.

If you receive another state benefit or can show that paying the fee would cause undue hardship because of the exceptional circumstances of your case, you may not have to pay a fee. If any of the above apply to you, you can obtain an application for an exemption from the court.

Other information you will need

In addition to a certified copy of your marriage certificate, you will need further information in order to complete your divorce petition. This includes:

- You and your spouse's full names and present addresses.

- The names and dates of birth of all your children, and where they are at school if over 16.

- The last address you and your spouse lived at as husband and wife.

- You and your spouse's occupations.

- Information on any court proceedings involving your marriage, a child or property of the family.

- The fact you are basing the divorce on, with supporting details.

Completing the divorce petition

This Guide contains completed examples of the forms you need to handle your own divorce. A divorce County court (or the Principal Registry) can provide you with the blank forms free of charge. They are also available online at the Court Service website: www.courtservice.gov.uk.

The first form you will complete is the *Divorce Petition (Form D8)*. You will need three copies of this form, and a fourth if you are naming someone as a co-respondent in a divorce based on adultery. The copies are distributed as follows:

(a) One for your records (keep copies of any forms or correspondence you send to the court or your spouse throughout the divorce proceedings).

(b) One for the court's records.

(c) One for the court to send to your spouse advising him or her of the divorce action.

(d) One for a co-respondent in an adultery case where applicable.

If you have children, you must also file three copies of the *Statement of Arrangements for Children (Form D8A)*.

Read the petition *Notes for Guidance* in this Guide. These will aid you further in completing your *Petition* and the *Statement of Arrangements for Children*. If you delete a numbered paragraph on a form, you should renumber those paragraphs that follow. However, do not delete any parts of the *Prayer* on the third page of *Form D8*, even if you think they are not required.

If you need further assistance, the staff of a divorce County court or a Citizens Advice Bureau can help.

Step 3. Serve your spouse

With your *Divorce Petition* and *Statement of Arrangements for Children* completed, the next step is serving your spouse with these forms. Sending the *Petition* and *Statement of Arrangements for Children* to your spouse is the responsibility of the court. It is your responsibility to provide the court with the correct address.

Leave two copies of the *Petition* and *Statement of Arrangements for Children* with the court, one for the court records and one for your spouse. The court will send copies of the *Petition* with an *Acknowledgment of Service* and *Notice of Proceedings.* These inform the respondent of the consequences of his or her responses, and ascertain the respondent's consent, sense of financial obligation, suggestions for alternate arrangements for children, etc.

About a week after you file your petition, the court will send you a *Notice of Issue of Petition* advising you that the petition has, in fact, been sent to your spouse, acknowledging that you have paid any filing fees, and informing you of your divorce case number. Keep this number for future reference. Now you simply await your spouse's response.

Step 4. Handle the response

Once your divorce petition is posted to your spouse, one of three events occurs:

- Your spouse does not respond to the petition, either because it was not delivered or because he or she ignored it.

- Your spouse indicates that he or she intends to contest the divorce.

- Your spouse indicates that he or she agrees with the divorce petition and wants a divorce.

This is how you should proceed in each instance:

Your spouse does not reply to the petition

If the *Acknowledgment of Service* is not returned, it may be because:

(a) Your spouse did not receive the petition.

If the petition was undeliverable, the court will send you a *Notice of Non-Service of Petition*. If the post office returns the petition to the court, it is your responsibility to obtain your spouse's correct address and notify the court so the petition may be successfully delivered.

(b) Your spouse chooses, for a variety of reasons, to ignore the petition.

The respondent has eight days from the day after receipt of the petition to return the *Acknowledgment of Service*. This time is extended if your spouse lives outside the country. If the *Acknowledgment* is not returned, you can arrange with the court for the petition and other documents to be served personally, by any disinterested third party, by the bailiff in the respondent's county, or by a process server. There is a service fee for using the bailiff or process server. Provide a recent close-up photograph or written description of your spouse or a co-respondent who does not acknowledge service of the divorce petition.

Your spouse acknowledges service and intends to defend against divorce

Divorces are seldom contested today, but it can occur. If your spouse acknowledges service, check his or her answer to the question, 'Do you intend to defend the case?'

If the answer is 'no', proceed to step 5.

If the answer is 'yes', you have a contested divorce and you must follow these two steps:

(a) Your spouse has 29 days from the date he or she received the petition (as marked on the *Acknowledgment of Service*) to file a defence to the divorce. If you receive a defence to the divorce, you should consult a solicitor to represent you, as proceedings from this point onward can be technical. To encourage your spouse to agree to divorce, you may seek an order for costs in the *Prayer* in the *Divorce Petition*.

(b) If you do not receive a defence within 29 days, you can ask the court for an application for directions for trial. This procedure is discussed below.

Your spouse acknowledges service and does not intend to contest the divorce

If your spouse answers 'no' to the question 'Do you intend to defend the case?', you can immediately apply for directions for trial.

You follow the same process if your spouse states an intent to contest or defend the divorce but does not file a written defence within 29 days. Therefore, it is only when your spouse duly files an answer to a contested divorce within 29 days that you cannot apply for directions for trial. In all other instances you may.

Step 5. Apply for directions for trial

By applying for directions for trial, you are asking the court to rule whether:

(a) the reasons stated in your petition are sufficient for the divorce to be granted;

(b) your proposed arrangements for the financial and residential care of your children, if any, are satisfactory.

You need to complete and send to the court an *Application for Directions for Trial (Form D84)* and an *Affidavit (Form D80)* in support of the petition that relates to the fact or facts you are proving for your divorce. There is no fee. (Completed examples of *Form D84* and a *Form D80* for each fact – adultery, unreasonable behaviour, desertion, two-year separation, five-year separation – are provided in this Guide.)

These forms may also be sent to the petitioner by the court when it sends the respondent's signed *Acknowledgment of Service*.

The petitioner must return the *Application for Directions for Trial* and the *Affidavit*, and identify the signatures on the *Statement of Arrangements for Children* and *Acknowledgment of Service* as that of the respondent.

Because *Form D80* is an affidavit, the individual who is asked to witness the petitioner's signature must see you sign and hear your declaration that your statement is true. Your witness to the *Affidavit* can be a solicitor or any officer of the court. There may be a nominal fee for this service if you use a solicitor.

You must answer in full both the *Application for Directions for Trial* and the *Affidavit*. Leave no blank spaces.

Along with *Forms D84* and *D80*, the court must have evidence that:

(a)   your spouse (and any named co-respondent) duly received your divorce petition;

(b)   your spouse admits to adultery where adultery is the fact relied on for divorce;

(c)   your spouse admits to unreasonable behaviour where unreasonable behaviour is the fact relied on for divorce;

(d)   your spouse admits to desertion where desertion is the fact relied on for divorce;

(e)   your spouse consents to the divorce where the fact relied on is that you lived apart for two or more years;

(f)   your spouse agrees to the proposed arrangements for children.

The *Acknowledgment of Service* will contain most if not all the above information that applies in your case. A copy of the *Statement of Arrangements for Children* will supply the information required in 6.

Step 6. Complete Form E

If you are asking the court to make orders about property, pensions or other financial matters, you must complete Form E to be filed with the court. You will find a note about the completion of Form E on page 39.

Step 7. Apply for your decree nisi

About two months after you file your *Application for Directions for Trial* and *Affidavit*, the court puts your case on the Special Procedure List, meaning the list of uncontested divorces. You are notified of the exact date that your case will come up a week or two in advance. If it is undefended, you needn't attend the court.

At that time your complete file is examined by the judge, who will consider:

(a) whether your documents are satisfactorily completed;

(b) whether you state proper grounds for divorce;

(c) whether the proposed arrangements for your children are in their best interests.

The court may request that you and your spouse appear if there is some minor question concerning the arrangements for the children or another small difficulty that is likely to be resolved by having an informal meeting. Attendance is also required if the decree or any court orders are opposed. You will know of this beforehand.

Occasionally, the judge will feel that there is a serious question concerning your entitlement to a divorce. Your case will then be removed from the Special Procedure List and entered on the undefended list. Should this occur, you will have to appear at a scheduled hearing. It is recommended that a solicitor accompanies you.

If the judge finds that your documents are in order and that you are entitled to a divorce, the court will send you and your spouse (and any co-respondent) certificates of entitlement to a decree nisi (or a decree of judicial separation, if that is what you filed for). If you have children, you will also receive a notice of satisfaction with the arrangements for children.

The judge also sets a date for granting, or 'pronouncing', a decree nisi. Again, you are not usually expected to appear in court on that date.

The decree nisi period

A decree nisi means that you are provisionally granted a divorce unless there are events that revoke or undo the decree before the divorce is finalised with a *Decree of Divorce Absolute*. During this period, the court can still decide that you are not entitled to a divorce (if, for instance, you falsified your *Affidavit*).

During this decree nisi period you are still legally married. Reconciling with your spouse would terminate the divorce proceedings. Should there be a late reconciliation, you should attempt to get your divorce petition and decree nisi dismissed by mutual consent. This is obviously more sensible than divorcing only to remarry.

You can ask the court to dismiss your petition whenever you believe the reconciliation is successful. Courts gladly promote the continuity of a harmonious marriage.

Your *Affidavit* asks whether, since the event on which you are basing your divorce, you have lived together with your spouse for any period totalling more than six months. The effect of periods of reconciliation depends on which fact for divorce you are using.

Fact A: Adultery and intolerability

You cannot obtain a divorce on the basis of adultery if you have lived for a total of more than six months with your spouse after discovering the adulterous act you cite in your petition. If the adultery continues into the present, cite the most recent instance. You must also confirm that you find it intolerable to live with your husband or wife, in view of his or her adultery.

Fact B: Unreasonable behaviour

In your *Affidavit* you should state the most recent incident of unreasonable behaviour. If you live with your spouse for fewer than six months after that, the period is ignored. Any period greater than six months does not stop you from obtaining a divorce, but the judge may weigh just how unreasonable the cited behaviour is.

If you think there will be a problem in the divorce process due to a period of reconciliation, consider citing a later instance of the fact on which you are basing the divorce, or consider citing another fact.

Facts C, D and E: Desertion, two- and five-year separations

Since these periods of separation are supposed to be continuous, any period of living together greater than six months means the two- or five-year separation must start again. If the period spent together is less than six months, the separation does not have to start again, but the reconciliation time cannot be counted towards the two- or five-year goal.

Application for the decree nisi is an important step in the divorce proceedings and should be handled with care, but a decree nisi is rarely refused by the court. Should it happen, you will be advised by the court with a notice of refusal of the judge's certificate. The form will state the reason for the refusal and the additional information needed before the decree nisi can be granted.

Your decree nisi will be sent by the court to you and your spouse (and any co-respondent) shortly after the judge decides that you have satisfied the requirements for divorce. If you requested that your spouse (or any co-respondent) pays your costs, you will also receive an *Order Supplementary to Decree Nisi.*

You cannot apply for a decree absolute until six weeks and one day have passed since your decree nisi was pronounced.

Step 8. Obtain your decree absolute

It is important to understand that you are not divorced until your decree absolute is issued.

It is easy to apply for your decree absolute. You file a *Notice of Application for Decree Nisi to be made Absolute (Form D36)* with the court. A completed example of *Form D36* is provided in this Guide. The filing fee is currently £30, unless you are exempt from fees.

Upon receiving your *Notice of Application for Decree Nisi to be made Absolute*, the court will verify that:

(a)   six weeks and one day have elapsed since the decree nisi;

(b)   the court is satisfied with the arrangements for the children;

(c)   there are no other reasons for denial of your decree absolute.

You, your spouse and any named co-respondent will be sent *Decrees Absolute* by the court, which officially end your marriage. Keep your decree absolute with your other important documents.

Post-divorce checklist

Once divorced, there are some basic steps you and your spouse must take so you can separate as cleanly as possible both financially and legally:

(a) Obtain from the court your decree absolute. You may need this to transfer property, divide bank accounts, etc.

(b) Resolve division of household contents as soon as possible. They may otherwise 'disappear,' no matter what your agreement says.

(c) Close any joint bank and savings accounts.

(d) Estimate utility bills if you do not have a final bill.

(e) If you have not yet done so, destroy or surrender to the issuer all joint credit and charge cards and notify the credit card companies that you no longer have responsibility for new debts of your former spouse. Open new accounts in your name alone and with a change of address, if applicable.

Glossary

A-C

Abduction – unlawful kidnapping.

Acknowledgment of Service – a form sent with the divorce petition to the respondent. When the form is completed and returned, receipt of the petition is acknowledged and service is complete.

Affidavit – a written 'statement of fact' made on oath and signed in the presence of an authorised person (e.g. solicitor). Used as evidence.

Ancillary relief – a maintenance arrangement that is supplementary to the divorce petition.

Arrangements for children – a plan for minor children, determined by the parents or by the court, detailing their living arrangements, health and welfare following a divorce.

Child support – financial maintenance of minor children by one or both parents.

Child Support Agency (CSA) – an organisation created by the Child Support Act 1991 that calculates and collects maintenance payments for children.

Children Act 1989 – legislation that, among other things, gives primary responsibility for minor children to both parents equally.

Clean break – a final settlement of financial and property matters so that neither party is dependent on the other. Virtually impossible if there are dependant children of the marriage.

Conciliation – an attempt to agree on the issues of the divorce without arguing them in court. Appointments may be made to see a conciliation officer at court. The parties may also agree things between themselves.

Contested divorce – occurs when the respondent does not agree to the divorce; also known as a defended divorce.

Co-respondent – in a divorce based on adultery, the person with whom the respondent is alleged to have committed adultery.

C–M

Cross-petition – a petition by the respondent in a divorce proceeding alleging different reasons for the divorce than those originally stated by the petitioner.

Decree absolute – final order of court to dissolve the marriage.

Decree nisi – in English, decree 'unless'; a provisional, not final, order of divorce.

Defended divorce – see Contested divorce.

Divorce – legal termination of a marriage on the ground that it has irretrievably broken down. This is proved by one or more of five facts.

Fact – one of five conditions – adultery, unreasonable behaviour, desertion, two-year and five-year separation – that prove that a marriage has broken down.

In chambers – in private; almost all divorce proceedings are heard this way.

Injunction – a court order for someone to refrain from doing something.

Interim court order – temporary orders made by a court pending the final divorce decree.

Judicial separation – a decree of the court that pronounces two parties legally separate without dissolving the marriage. Can include financial settlement.

Jurisdiction – the authority of courts to deal with a case. English courts have jurisdiction for divorce if the domicile and/or residence qualifications are fulfilled.

Legal Aid – was advice or assistance provided to those who qualify at reduced rates or no charge. Now called public funding.

Maintenance – financial support given by one party to the other during and after a divorce. Can be in the form of regular payments (monthly, yearly) or a lump sum.

Maintenance pending suit – a temporary court order for one spouse to provide financial support to the other pending the final divorce decree.

M–S

Mediation – intervention by a trained, impartial third party when couples need help to find their own solutions in disagreements about children, finance or property.

Non-molestation injunction – a court order preventing the estranged spouse from interfering with the carer spouse and the children.

Orders for residence and contact – court orders establishing where minor children will live and who may visit them.

Ouster injunction – a court order preventing an abusive spouse from entering the home of the carer spouse and the children.

Petitioner – the party who starts the proceedings leading to divorce by completing a form and ensuring it is received by the respondent.

Prayer – the application at the end of the petition asking for the marriage to be dissolved, for financial relief to be ordered and for orders relating to children, if appropriate.

Register a charge – an action protecting a spouse's interest in the matrimonial home when the other spouse is sole owner.

Resident parent – the parent having day-to-day responsibility for the minor children following a divorce.

Respondent – the person who receives the petition for divorce.

Separation – an agreement or legal decree releasing spouses from the duty to cohabit.

Service – the act of presenting a spouse with a document (e.g. a divorce petition) so that delivery and receipt can be proved.

Special Procedure – the normal process for a simple, undefended divorce, which the majority of divorces are.

Specific issue order – order settling disputes on issues relating to children.

Status quo – the existing situation.

Appendix

Addresses

**British Association for
Counselling and Psychotherapy**
BACP House
35–37 Albert Street
Rugby CV21 2SG
Tel: 0870 443 5252
Email: bacp@bacp.co.uk
Website: www.bacp.co.uk

The Child Abduction Unit
81 Chancery Lane
London WC2A 1DD
Tel: 020 7911 7047
Email: enquiries@offsol.gsi.
gov.uk
Website: www.offsol.demon.co.uk/
caunitfm.htm

Child Poverty Action Group
94 White Lion Street
London N1 9PF
Tel: 020 7837 7979
Email: staff@cpag.org.uk
Website: www.cpag.org.uk

The Children's Society
Edward Rudolf House
Margery Street
London WC1X 0JL
Tel: 0845 300 1128
Email: supporteraction@
childrenssociety.org.uk
Website: www.the-childrens-
society.org.uk

Citizens Advice Bureau
The address and telephone
number of your local bureau
is in the telephone book
under 'Citizens'.

**Divorce, Mediation &
Counselling Service**
38 Ebury Street
London SW1W 0LU
Tel: 020 7730 2422

Families Need Fathers
134 Curtain Road
London EC2A 3AR
Tel: 0870 760 7496
Email: fnf@fnf.org.uk
Website: www.fnf.org.uk

Family Mediation Scotland
18 York Place
Edinburgh EH1 3EP
Tel: 0131 558 9898
Email: info@familymediation
scotland.org.uk
Website: www.familymediation
scotland.org.uk

Family Rights Group
The Print House
18 Ashwin Street
London E8 3DL
Tel: 0800 731 1696
Email: office@frg.org.uk
Website: www.frg.org.uk

Foreign and Commonwealth Office
Child Abduction Unit
Consular Directorate
Old Admiralty Building
London SW1A 2PA
Tel: 020 7008 8737/020 7008 0200
Website: www.fco.gov.uk

Gingerbread
7 Sovereign Close
Sovereign Court
London E1W 2HW
Tel: 0800 018 4318
Email: office@gingerbread.org.uk
Website: www.gingerbread.org.uk

Jewish Marriage Council
23 Ravenshurst Avenue
London NW4 4EE
Tel: 020 8203 6311
Email: info@jmc-uk.org
Website: www.jmc-uk.org

Land Charges Department
Plumer House
Tailyour Road
Crownhill
Plymouth PL6 5HY
Tel: 01752 636 666
Website: www.landreg.gov.uk

Land Registry
Lincoln's Inn Fields
London WC2A 3PH
Tel: 020 7917 8888
Email: enquiries.pic@land registry.gov.uk
Website: www.landreg.gov.uk

The Law Society
113 Chancery Lane
London WC2A 1PL
Tel: 020 7242 1222
Website: www.lawsociety.org.uk

Legal Action Group
242 Pentonville Road
London N1 9UN
Tel: 020 7833 2931
Email: lag@lag.org.uk
Website: www.lag.org.uk

Legal Services Commission
85 Gray's Inn Road
London WC1X 8TX
Tel: 020 7759 0000
Website: www.legalservices.gov.uk

Lothian Family Mediation Service
37 George Street
Edinburgh EH2 2HN
Tel: 0131 226 4507
Email: lothian@familymediation. freeserve.co.uk
Website: www.familymediation scotland.org.uk

Marriage Care
1 Blythe Mews
Blythe Road
London W14 0NW
Tel: 020 7371 1341
Email: info@marriagecare.org.uk
Website: www.marriagecare.org.uk

National Debtline
The Arch
48–52 Floodgate Street
Birmingham B5 5SL
Tel: 0808 808 4000
Website: www.nationaldebtline. co.uk

National Family Mediation
Alexander House
Telephone Avenue
Bristol BS1 4BS
Tel: 0117 904 2825
Email: general@nfm.org.uk
Website: www.nfm.u-net.com

National Federation of Solo Clubs
PO Box 2278
Nuneaton
Warks. CV11 5PA
Tel: 024 7673 6499
Website: www.federation-solo-clubs.co.uk

One Parent Families
255 Kentish Town Road
London NW5 2LX
Tel: 0800 018 5026
Email: info@oneparentfamilies.org.uk
Website: www.oneparentfamilies.org.uk

Parentline Plus (formerly The National Stepfamily Association)
520 Highgate Studios
53–79 Highgate Road
London NW5 1TL
Tel: 0808 800 2222
Email: centraloffice@parentlineplus.org.uk
Website: www.parentlineplus.org.uk

Professional Classes Aid Council
10 St. Christopher's Place
London W1U 1HZ
Tel: 020 7935 0641
Email: admin@pcac.org.uk
Website: www.pcac.org.uk

Relate Marriage Guidance
See their website for the address of your local branch.
Tel: 0845 130 4016
Email: enquiries@relate.org.uk
Website: www.relate.org.uk

Reunite
International Child Abduction Centre
PO Box 7124
Leicester LE1 7XX
Tel: 0116 255 6234
Email: reunite@dircon.co.uk
Website: www.reunite.org

Shelter
88 Old Street
London EC1V 9HU
Tel: 0808 800 4444
Email: info@shelter.org.uk
Website: www.shelter.org.uk

Solicitors Family Law Association
PO Box 302
Orpington
Kent BR6 8QX
Tel: 0168 985 0227
Email: info@sfla.org.uk
Website: www.sfla.org.uk

South East London Family Mediation Bureau
1st Floor, The Stables
1 North Street
Bromley BR1 1SD
Tel: 020 8315 7460

The United Kingdom Passport Office
Globe House
89 Eccleston Square
London SW1V 1PN

Tel: 0870 521 0410
Website: www.ukpa.gov.uk

Women's Aid
PO Box 391
Bristol BS99 7WS
Tel: 0808 200 0247
Email: info@womensaid.org.uk
Website: www.womensaid.org.uk

The forms

You should obtain copies of the forms you need from your local County court, listed in the telephone directory. They can also be obtained at their website address www.courtservice.gov.uk.

Notes for Guidance 119

Completed examples of *Form D8*, Divorce Petition

    Adultery   122

    Unreasonable Behaviour 127

    Desertion   132

    Two-Year Separation 137

    Five-Year Separation 142

Completed example of *Form D8A*
Statement of Arrangements for Children   147

Completed examples of *Form D80*, Affidavit of Evidence

    Adultery   155

    Unreasonable Behaviour 159

    Desertion   163

    Two-Year Separation 167

    Five-Year Separation 171

Completed example of *Form D84*
Application for Directions for Trial 175

Completed example of *Form D36*, Notice of
Application for Decree Nisi to be made Absolute 176

Blank example of *Form E*, Financial Statement   177

Blank example of Deed of Separation   197

Any other forms required as your divorce proceedings continue will be supplied to you by the court. You are responsible for obtaining a certified copy of your marriage certificate, which will not be returned to you.

Form D8, Divorce Petition

If you fill out the petition to start the divorce, you are the petitioner. Completed sample petitions citing each of the five facts that prove the grounds for divorce (adultery, unreasonable behaviour, desertion and two-year and five-year separation) are provided in this Guide. The Divorce Petition Notes will help you to fill out your petition and prayer.

Form D8A, Statement of Arrangements for Children

Use this form if you or the respondent have minor children who will be affected by the divorce.

Form D80, Affidavit

Five completed examples of the affidavit are found in this Guide. *Forms D80(a)* to *D80(e)* coincide with the five facts for divorce. Be sure to use the *Form D80* that correlates to the facts used to support the ground for your divorce petition:

D80(a) Adultery

D80(b) Unreasonable behaviour

D80(c) Desertion

D80(d) Two-year separation

D80(e) Five-year separation

Form D84, Application for Directions for Trial

Use this form if your divorce petition is uncontested by the respondent. Along with this application, file your corresponding affidavit.

Form D36, Notice of Application for Decree Nisi to be made Absolute

You can file this notice with the court six weeks and a day after your Decree Nisi is granted but you may wish to leave it longer if financial matters have not been resolved.

Form E, Financial Statement

This has to be filed if you are asking for any orders about property, income or pensions. Unless your financial position is extremely simple, you should get a qualified family mediator/solicitor to help you complete it.

Deed of Separation

This template relates to the final terms of separation only; if necessary, you can agree interim terms and place those into an interim deed of separation if you wish. It would be prudent to at least obtain initial legal advice before proceeding to draw up a deed of separation, because otherwise the agreement may not be upheld in court.

Divorce Petition Notes for Guidance

Each of the notes below will help you to complete that paragraph in the divorce petition which has the same number as the note. You should not cross out any of the paragraphs numbered 1 to 13 unless the notes say that you should.

(1) You will find the information you need to complete this paragraph on your marriage certificate. You must explain any differences between the information given in your petition and that on your marriage certificate.

If either you or the respondent have changed your name(s) since the marriage took place you must explain this, for example by adding:

- name changed by deed poll,
- now known as.

Please give:

- the date of your marriage,
- your full name (the petitioner)
- the full name of your husband or wife (the respondent)
- the place of the marriage.

When giving the place of marriage you should write the words – both printed and hand-written – contained in the marriage certificate which come after the phrase "Marriage solemnised at", for example:

Where the marriage took place in a Register Office:

The Register Office, in the District of ....
in the County of ....

Where the marriage took place in a church:

.... Church, in the Parish of ....
in the County of ....

(2) Please give the last address at which you have lived with the respondent as husband and wife.

(3) Please write in, exactly as set out below, the following paragraph (or paragraphs) upon which you intend to rely to prove that the court has jurisdiction under Article 2(1) of the Council Regulation and therefore may deal with your petition. If you are completing this form without a solicitor and need help deciding which paragraph(s) applies, a Citizens Advice Bureau will be able to help you.

(a) "The petitioner and respondent are both habitually resident in England and Wales."

(b) "The petitioner and respondent were last habitually resident in England and Wales and the *[petitioner] [respondent] still resides there." (*Delete as appropriate)

(c) "The respondent is habitually resident in England and Wales."

(d) "The petitioner is habitually resident in England and Wales and has resided there for at least one year immediately prior to the presentation of this petition." (You should give the address(es) where you lived during that time and the length of time lived at each address.)

(e) "The petitioner is domiciled and habitually resident in England and Wales and has resided there for at least six months immediately prior to the presentation of the petition." (You should give the address(es) where you lived during that time and the length of time lived at each address.)

(f) "The petitioner and the respondent are both domiciled in England and Wales."

If none of the above paragraphs apply to you but you believe that the court still has jurisdiction to deal with your petition, cross out the words "The court has jurisdiction under Article 2(1) of the Council Regulation on the following ground(s):" and add the following paragraph, if it applies:

"The court has jurisdiction other than under Council Regulation on the basis that no Contracting State has jurisdiction under the Council Regulation and the *[petitioner] [respondent] is domiciled in England and Wales on the date when this petition is issued."
(*Delete as appropriate)

(4) Please give your occupation and current address and those of the respondent.

(5) If there are no children of the family cross out the word "except". If there are any children of the family give:

- their full names (including surname),
- their date of birth, or if over 18 say so,
- if the child is over 16 but under 18, say if he or she is at school, or college,

  or

  is training for a trade, profession or vocation,

  or

  is working full time.

(6) If no other child has been born during the marriage you should cross out the word "except".

If you are the husband, cross out the word "petitioner" where it first appears in the paragraph, but do not cross out the words in brackets

If you are the wife, cross out the word "respondent", and cross out the words in brackets.

D8 (Notes)

If there is a child give:

- the full name (including surname),
- the date of birth, or if over 18 say so.

If there is a dispute whether a living child is a child of the family please add a paragraph saying so.

(7) If there have not been any court proceedings in England and Wales or elsewhere concerning:

- your marriage,
- any child of the family,
- any property belonging to either you or the respondent

cross out the word "except".

If there have been proceedings please give:

- the name of the court in which they took place,
- details of the order(s) which were made,
- if the proceedings were about your marriage say
  if you and the respondent resumed living together as husband and wife after the order was made.

(8) If there have not been any proceedings in the Child Support Agency concerning the maintenance of any child of the family, cross out the word "except".

If there have been any proceedings please give

- the date of any application to the Agency
- details of the calculation made.

(9) If there have been no proceedings in a court outside England and Wales which have affected the marriage, or may affect it, cross out the word "except".

If there are or have been proceedings please give:

- the name of the country and the court in which they are taking/have taken place,
- the date the proceedings were begun and the names of the parties,
- details of the order(s) made,
- if no order has yet been made, the date of any future hearing.

(10) If your petition is not based on five years' separation, cross out this paragraph.

If your petition is based on five year's separation but no agreement or arrangement has been made, cross out the word "except".

If your petition is based on five years, separation and an agreement or arrangement has been made with the respondent:

- about maintenance either for him or herself or for any child of the family,
- about the family property,

please give full details.

(11) If you are applying for a judicial separation please cross out this paragraph.

(12) Please write in, exactly as set out below, the paragraph (or paragraphs) upon which you intend to rely to prove that your marriage has irretrievably broken down.

(a) The respondent has committed adultery with a [man] [woman] and the petitioner finds it intolerable to live with the respondent.

or

The respondent has committed adultery [with (give the name) .... (called the co-respondent)] and the petitioner finds it intolerable to live with the respondent.

(b) The respondent has behaved in such a way that the petitioner cannot reasonably be expected to live with the respondent.

(c) The respondent has deserted the petitioner for a continuous period of at least two years immediately preceding the presentation of this petition.

(d) The parties to the marriage have lived apart for a continuous period of at least two years immediately preceding the presentation of the petition and the respondent consents to a decree being granted.

(e) The parties to the marriage have lived apart for a continuous period of at least five years immediately preceding the presentation of the petition.

Please note: *You do not need to give the name of the person with whom the respondent has committed adultery unless you wish to claim costs against that person.*

Particulars

(13) This space is provided for you to give details of the allegations which you are using to prove the facts given in paragraph 12. In most cases one or two sentences will do.

(a) If you have alleged adultery give:

- the date(s) and place(s) where the adultery took place.

(b) If you have alleged unreasonable behaviour give:

- details of particular incidents, including dates, but it should not be necessary to give more than about half a dozen examples of the more serious incidents, including the most recent.

(c) If you have alleged desertion give:

- the date of desertion
- brief details of how the desertion came about.

(d) & (e) If you have alleged either two or five year's separation give:

- the date of separation,
- brief details of how the separation came about.

Prayer

The prayer of the petition is your request to the court. You should consider carefully the claims which you wish to make.

You should adapt the prayer to suit your claims.

(1) The suit

If you are asking for a judicial separation, cross out this paragraph and write in its place:

"That the petitioner may be judicially separated from the respondent".

(2) Costs

If you wish to claim that the respondent or co-respondent pay your costs you must do so in your petition.

It is not possible to make a claim after a decree has been granted.

If you do wish to claim costs write in respondent, or co-respondent, or both, as appropriate.

If you do not wish to claim costs, cross out this paragraph.

(3) Ancillary relief

If you wish to apply for any of these orders, complete paragraph 3 by deleting those orders you do not require.

You are advised to see a solicitor if you are unsure about which order(s) you require.

If you cross out this paragraph, or any part of it, and later change your mind, you will first have to ask the court's permission before any application can be made. Permission cannot be granted after re-marriage.

If you apply in the prayer for an order you must complete Form A when you are ready to proceed with your application.

If you are asking for a property adjustment order, give the address of the property concerned.

If you are asking for a pension sharing or attachment order, give details of the order you require.

You can apply to the court for ancillary relief for children if you are asking for one or more of the following:

- a lump sum payment,
- * settlement of property,
- * transfer of property,
- * secured periodical payments,
- financial provision for a stepchild or stepchildren
of the respondent.

These orders can only be made in the High Court or a county court.

- periodical payments when either the child or, the person with care of the child, or

  the absent parent of the child is **not** habitually resident in the United Kingdom,

- periodical payments in addition to child support maintenance paid under a Child Support Agency calculation,

- periodical payments to meet expenses arising from a child's disability,

- periodical payments to meet expenses incurred by a child in being educated or training for work.

If none of the above applies to you, you should make an application for child maintenance to the Child Support Agency; the court cannot make an order for child maintenance in your case. A leaflet about the Child Support Agency is available from any court office.

If you are not sure whether the court can hear your application please ask a member of the court staff. A leaflet 'I want to apply for a financial order' is also available.

Finally, do not forget to

- sign and date the petition,

- give the name(s) and personal address(es) of the person(s) to be served with the petition,

- bring or send your marriage certificate and fee to the court,

- complete a Statement of Arrangements if there are children of the family.

Arrangements for Children

If you consider that the court will need to:

- determine where the child(ren) should live (a Residence Order),

- determine with whom the child(ren) should have contact (a Contact Order),

- make a Specific Issue Order,

- make a Prohibited Steps Order,

you must apply for the order form C2.

You may enclose the completed form with your petition or submit it later. If you wish to apply for any of these orders, or any other orders which may be available to you under part I or II of the Children Act 1989, you are advised to see a solicitor.

The Court will only make an order if it considers that an order will be better for the child(ren) than no order.

All forms and leaflets are available from your Court.

Completed example of Form D8 Divorce Petition (Adultery)

Before completing this form, read carefully the attached **Notes for Guidance**.

In the Doncaster

~~**In the Principal Registry***~~

County Court*

*Delete as appropriate

No.

(1)   On the 1st   day of   June   [~~19——~~] [20 02] the petitioner

Jane Brown   was lawfully married to

David Brown   (hereinafter called "the

respondent") at   St. Stephen's Church, Old Church Street, London, SW6

(2)   The petitioner and respondent last lived together as husband and wife at

"Cosy Nook", Doncaster, South Yorkshire

(3)   The court has jurisdiction under Article 2(1) of the Council Regulation on the following ground(s):

The petitioner and the respondent are both habitually resident in England and Wales.

(4)   The petitioner is by occupation a   Nurse   and resides at

"Cosy Nook", Doncaster, South Yorkshire

The respondent is by occupation a   Sales Executive   and resides at

Flat 51, Belvedere Drive, Sheffield

(5)   There are no children of the family now living *except*

James Brown who was born on 19th October 2003

(6)   No other child, now living, has been born to the petitioner/~~respondent~~ during the marriage (~~so far as is known to the petitioner) except~~

(7)   There are or have been no other proceedings in any court in England and Wales or elsewhere with reference to the marriage (or to any child of the family) or between the petitioner and respondent with reference to any property of either or both of them ~~except~~

(8)   There are or have been no proceedings in the Child Support Agency with reference to the maintenance of any child of the family ~~except~~

(9)   There are no proceedings continuing in any country outside England or Wales which are in respect of the marriage or are capable of affecting its validity or subsistence ~~except~~

~~(10)   (This paragraph should be completed only if the petition is based on five years' separation.) No agreement or arrangement has been made or is proposed to be made between the parties for the support of the petitioner/respondent (and any child of the family) except~~

(10)
~~(11)~~   The said marriage has broken down irretrievably.

(11)
~~(12)~~   The respondent has committed adultery with a woman and the petitioner finds it intolerable to live with the respondent.

(12)
(13) **Particulars**

On Monday the 4th of June 2004 at Flat 72, Upper Park Road, Leeds, the respondent committed adultery.

Prayer

The petitioner therefore prays

(1) **The suit**

That the said marriage be dissolved

(2) **Costs**

That the   respondent   may be ordered to pay the costs of this suit if defended.

(3) **Ancillary relief**

That the petitioner may be granted the following ancillary relief:

(a)   an order for maintenance pending suit

a periodical payments order

a secured provision order

a lump sum order

a property adjustment order

an order under section 24B, 25B or 25C of the Act of 1973 (Pension Sharing/Attachment Order)

(b)   ~~For the children~~

~~a periodical payments order~~

~~a secured provision order~~

~~a lump sum order~~

~~a property adjustment order~~

Signed   *Jane Brown*

The names and addresses of the persons to be served with the petition are:

Respondent: David Brown
                Flat 51, Belvedere Drive, Sheffield

Co-Respondent (adultery case only):

The Petitioner's address for service is: Jane Brown
                                            "Cosy Nook", Doncaster, South Yorkshire

Dated this   16th   day of   September   20 04

Address all communications for the court to: The Court Manager, County Court,

The Court   }
office at   } Doncaster

is open from 10 a.m. to 4 p.m. (4.30 p.m. at the Principal Registry of the Family Division) on Mondays to Fridays.

Completed example of Form D8 Divorce Petition (Adultery) (continued)

In the

Doncaster   County Court*

No.

~~In the Principal Registry*~~

Between   Jane Brown

Petitioner

and

David Brown   Respondent

Divorce Petition

Full name and address of the petitioner or
of solicitors if they are acting for the petitioner.

Jane Brown
"Cosy Nook"
Doncaster
South Yorkshire

Completed example of Form D8 Divorce Petition (Unreasonable Behaviour)

Before completing this form, read carefully the attached **Notes for Guidance**.

In the   Doncaster   **County Court***
                                                            *Delete as
                                                            appropriate

~~**In the Principal Registry***~~   **No.**

(1)   On the 1st   day of   June   [19 99] ~~[20   ]~~ the petitioner

       Jane Brown   was lawfully married to

       David Brown   (hereinafter called "the

       respondent") at   St. Stephen's Church, Old Church Street, London, SW6

(2)   The petitioner and respondent last lived together as husband and wife at

       "Cosy Nook", Doncaster, South Yorkshire

(3)   The court has jurisdiction under Article 2(1) of the Council Regulation on the following ground(s):

       The petitioner and the respondent are both habitually resident in England and Wales.

(4)   The petitioner is by occupation a   Nurse   and resides at

       "Cosy Nook", Doncaster, South Yorkshire

       The respondent is by occupation a Sales Executive   and resides at

       Flat 51, Belvedere Drive, Sheffield

(5)   There are no children of the family now living ~~except~~

(6)   No other child, now living, has been born to the petitioner/~~respondent~~ during the marriage (~~so far as is known to the petitioner) except~~

D8 (9.01)   *Printed on behalf of the Court Service*

(7)   There are or have been no other proceedings in any court in England and Wales or elsewhere with reference to the marriage (or to any child of the family) or between the petitioner and respondent with reference to any property of either or both of them ~~except~~

(8)   There are or have been no proceedings in the Child Support Agency with reference to the maintenance of any child of the family ~~except~~

(9)   There are no proceedings continuing in any country outside England or Wales which are in respect of the marriage or are capable of affecting its validity or subsistence ~~except~~

(10)   ~~(This paragraph should be completed only if the petition is based on five years' separation.)~~
       ~~No agreement or arrangement has been made or is proposed to be made between the parties for the support of~~
       ~~the petitioner/respondent (and any child of the family) except~~

(10)
~~(11)~~   The said marriage has broken down irretrievably.

(11)
~~(12)~~   The respondent has behaved in such a way that the petitioner cannot reasonably be expected to live with the respondent.

(12)
~~(13)~~ **Particulars**

A.   Throughout the marriage the respondent has consumed alcohol to excess, frequently causing embarrassment to the petitioner.

B.   On 12th April 2003, the respondent crashed the petitioner's car whilst drunk and the respondent has consequently lost his licence.

C.   The respondent refuses to have children which has caused great distress to the petitioner.

D.   The respondent has refused sexual intercourse with the petitioner since May 2003.

Prayer

The petitioner therefore prays

(1) **The suit**

That the said marriage be dissolved

(2) **Costs**

That the respondent may be ordered to pay the costs of this suit if defended.

(3) **Ancillary relief**

That the petitioner may be granted the following ancillary relief:

(a) an order for maintenance pending suit

a periodical payments order

a secured provision order

a lump sum order

a property adjustment order

an order under section 24B, 25B or 25C of the Act of 1973 (Pension Sharing/Attachment Order)

(b) ~~For the children~~

~~a periodical payments order~~

~~a secured provision order~~

~~a lump sum order~~

~~a property adjustment order~~

Signed *Jane Brown*

The names and addresses of the persons to be served with the petition are:

Respondent: David Brown
Flat 51, Belvedere Drive, Sheffield

Co-Respondent (adultery case only):

The Petitioner's address for service is: Jane Brown
"Cosy Nook", Doncaster, South Yorkshire

Dated this 16th day of September 20 04

Address all communications for the court to: The Court Manager, County Court,

The Court
office at } Doncaster

is open from 10 a.m. to 4 p.m. (4.30 p.m. at the Principal Registry of the Family Division) on Mondays to Fridays.

In the

Doncaster   County Court*

No.

~~In the Principal Registry~~*

Between   Jane Brown

Petitioner

and

David Brown   Respondent

Divorce Petition

Full name and address of the petitioner or
of solicitors if they are acting for the petitioner.

Jane Brown
"Cosy Nook"
Doncaster
South Yorkshire

Completed example of Form D8 Divorce Petition (Desertion)

Before completing this form, read carefully the attached **Notes for Guidance**.

In the   Doncaster   **County Court***

                                                          *Delete as appropriate

~~**In the Principal Registry***~~   **No.**

(1)   On the   1st   day of   June   [~~19~~] [20 00] the petitioner

David Brown   was lawfully married to

Jane Brown   (hereinafter called "the

respondent") at   St. Stephen's Church, Old Church Street, London, SW6

(2)   The petitioner and respondent last lived together as husband and wife at

"Cosy Nook", Doncaster, South Yorkshire

(3)   The court has jurisdiction under Article 2(1) of the Council Regulation on the following ground(s):

The petitioner and the respondent are both habitually resident in England and Wales.

(4)   The petitioner is by occupation a   Sales Executive   and resides at

"Cosy Nook", Doncaster, South Yorkshire

The respondent is by occupation a   Nurse   and resides at

Flat 51, Belvedere Drive, Sheffield

(5)   There are no children of the family now living *except*

James Brown who was born on 19th October 2001
Fiona Brown who was born on 19th October 2001

(6)   No other child, now living, has been born to the ~~petitioner~~/respondent during the marriage (so far as is known to the petitioner) ~~except~~

D8 (9.01)   *Printed on behalf of the Court Service*

Completed example of Form D8 Divorce Petition (Desertion) (continued)

(7) There are or have been no other proceedings in any court in England and Wales or elsewhere with reference to the marriage (or to any child of the family) or between the petitioner and respondent with reference to any property of either or both of them ~~except~~

(8) There are or have been no proceedings in the Child Support Agency with reference to the maintenance of any child of the family ~~except~~

(9) There are no proceedings continuing in any country outside England or Wales which are in respect of the marriage or are capable of affecting its validity or subsistence ~~except~~

(10) ~~(This paragraph should be completed only if the petition is based on five years' separation.) No agreement or arrangement has been made or is proposed to be made between the parties for the support of the petitioner/respondent (and any child of the family) except~~

(10)
~~(11)~~ The said marriage has broken down irretrievably.

(11)
~~(12)~~ The respondent has deserted the petitioner for a continuous period of at least two years immediately preceding the presentation of this petition.

133

(12)
(13) **Particulars**

On 2nd February 2002 the respondent left the petitioner without just cause and without the petitioner's consent with the intention of bringing cohabitation between the parties permanently to an end. The respondent has since not returned to live with the petitioner.

Prayer

The petitioner therefore prays

(1)   **The suit**

That the said marriage be dissolved

(2)   **Costs**

That the   respondent   may be ordered to pay the costs of this suit if defended.

(3)   **Ancillary relief**

That the petitioner may be granted the following ancillary relief:

(a)   an order for maintenance pending suit

a periodical payments order

a secured provision order

a lump sum order

a property adjustment order

an order under section 24B, 25B or 25C of the Act of 1973 (Pension Sharing/Attachment Order)

(b)   ~~For the children~~

~~a periodical payments order~~

~~a secured provision order~~

~~a lump sum order~~

~~a property adjustment order~~

Signed   *David Brown*

The names and addresses of the persons to be served with the petition are:

Respondent: Jane Brown
               Flat 51, Belvedere Drive, Sheffield

Co-Respondent (adultery case only):

The Petitioner's address for service is: David Brown
                                      "Cosy Nook", Doncaster, South Yorkshire

Dated this   16th   day of   September   20 04

Address all communications for the court to: The Court Manager, County Court,

The Court   }
office at   }   Doncaster

is open from 10 a.m. to 4 p.m. (4.30 p.m. at the Principal Registry of the Family Division) on Mondays to Fridays.

Completed example of Form D8 Divorce Petition (Desertion) (continued)

In the

Doncaster   County Court*

No.

~~In the Principal Registry~~*

Between   David Brown

Petitioner

and   Jane Brown

Respondent

Divorce Petition

Full name and address of the petitioner or
of solicitors if they are acting for the petitioner.

David Brown
"Cosy Nook"
Doncaster
South Yorkshire

Before completing this form, read carefully the attached **Notes for Guidance**.

In the   Doncaster   **County Court***

                                                                          *Delete as
                                                                          appropriate

~~**In the Principal Registry***~~   **No.**

(1)   On the 1st   day of   June   [19 99] [~~20   ~~] the petitioner

      David Brown   was lawfully married to

      Jane Brown   (hereinafter called "the

      respondent") at   St. Stephen's Church, Old Church Street, London, SW6

(2)   The petitioner and respondent last lived together as husband and wife at

      "Cosy Nook", Doncaster, South Yorkshire

(3)   The court has jurisdiction under Article 2(1) of the Council Regulation on the following ground(s):

      The petitioner and the respondent are both habitually resident in England and Wales.

(4)   The petitioner is by occupation a Sales Executive   and resides at

      "Cosy Nook", Doncaster, South Yorkshire

      The respondent is by occupation a   Nurse   and resides at

      Flat 51, Belvedere Drive, Sheffield

(5)   There are no children of the family now living ~~except~~

(6)   No other child, now living, has been born to the petitioner/~~respondent~~ during the marriage (so far as is known
      to the petitioner) ~~except~~

D8 (9.01)   *Printed on behalf of the Court Service*

(7)   There are or have been no other proceedings in any court in England and Wales or elsewhere with reference to the marriage (or to any child of the family) or between the petitioner and respondent with reference to any property of either or both of them ~~except~~

(8)   There are or have been no proceedings in the Child Support Agency with reference to the maintenance of any child of the family ~~except~~

(9)   There are no proceedings continuing in any country outside England or Wales which are in respect of the marriage or are capable of affecting its validity or subsistence ~~except~~

(10)   ~~(This paragraph should be completed only if the petition is based on five years' separation.)~~
~~No agreement or arrangement has been made or is proposed to be made between the parties for the support of~~
~~the petitioner/respondent (and any child of the family) except~~

(10)
~~(11)~~   The said marriage has broken down irretrievably.

(11)
~~(12)~~   The parties to the marriage have lived apart for a continuous period of at least two years immediately preceding the presentation of the petition and the respondent consents to a decree being granted.

(12)
~~(13)~~ **Particulars**

The petitioner and the respondent have lived apart since 1st January 2002 when the respondent left the matrimonial home at "Cosy Nook", Doncaster, South Yorkshire.

Prayer

The petitioner therefore prays

(1) **The suit**

That the said marriage be dissolved

(2) **Costs**

That the   respondent   may be ordered to pay the costs of this suit **if defended.**

(3) **Ancillary relief**

That the petitioner may be granted the following ancillary relief:

(a) an order for maintenance pending suit

a periodical payments order

a secured provision order

a lump sum order

a property adjustment order

an order under section 24B, 25B or 25C of the Act of 1973 (Pension Sharing/Attachment Order)

(b) ~~For the children~~

~~a periodical payments order~~

~~a secured provision order~~

~~a lump sum order~~

~~a property adjustment order~~

Signed   *David Brown*

The names and addresses of the persons to be served with the petition are:

Respondent: Jane Brown
Flat 51, Belvedere Drive, Sheffield

Co-Respondent (adultery case only):

The Petitioner's address for service is: David Brown
"Cosy Nook", Doncaster, South Yorkshire

Dated this   16th   day of   September   20 04

Address all communications for the court to: The Court Manager, County Court,

The Court   }
office at   }   Doncaster

is open from 10 a.m. to 4 p.m. (4.30 p.m. at the Principal Registry of the Family Division) on Mondays to Fridays.

In the

Doncaster   County Court*

No.

~~In the Principal Registry*~~

Between   David Brown

Petitioner

and   Jane Brown

Respondent

Divorce Petition

Full name and address of the petitioner or
of solicitors if they are acting for the petitioner.

David Brown
"Cosy Nook"
Doncaster
South Yorkshire

Completed example of Form D8 Divorce Petition (Five-Year Separation)

Before completing this form, read carefully the attached **Notes for Guidance**.

In the Doncaster

County Court*

*Delete as appropriate

~~**In the Principal Registry***~~

No.

(1) On the 1st day of June [19 94] [~~20~~] the petitioner

David Brown was lawfully married to

Jane Brown (hereinafter called "the

respondent") at St. Stephen's Church, Old Church Street, London, SW6

(2) The petitioner and respondent last lived together as husband and wife at

"Cosy Nook", Doncaster, South Yorkshire

(3) The court has jurisdiction under Article 2(1) of the Council Regulation on the following ground(s):

The petitioner and the respondent are both habitually resident in England and Wales.

(4) The petitioner is by occupation a **Sales Executive** and resides at

"Cosy Nook", Doncaster, South Yorkshire

The respondent is by occupation a **Nurse** and resides at

Flat 51, Belvedere Drive, Sheffield

(5) There are no children of the family now living *except*

James Brown who was born on 19th October 1995

(6) No other child, now living, has been born to the ~~petitioner~~/respondent during the marriage (so far as is known to the petitioner) ~~except~~

Printed on behalf of the Court Service

(7)   There are or have been no other proceedings in any court in England and Wales or elsewhere with reference to the marriage (or to any child of the family) or between the petitioner and respondent with reference to any property of either or both of them ~~except~~

(8)   There are or have been no proceedings in the Child Support Agency with reference to the maintenance of any child of the family ~~except~~

(9)   There are no proceedings continuing in any country outside England or Wales which are in respect of the marriage or are capable of affecting its validity or subsistence ~~except~~

(10)   (This paragraph should be completed only if the petition is based on five years' separation.)
        No agreement or arrangement has been made or is proposed to be made between the parties for the support of the petitioner/respondent (and any child of the family) ~~except~~

(11)   The said marriage has broken down irretrievably.

(12)   The parties to the marriage have lived apart for a continuous period of at least five years immediately preceding the presentation of the petition.

(13) **Particulars**

The parties to the marriage have lived apart since 12th January 1999 when the respondent left the matrimonial home at "Cosy Nook", Doncaster, South Yorkshire, since which date they have not resumed cohabitation.

Prayer

The petitioner therefore prays

(1) **The suit**

That the said marriage be dissolved

(2) **Costs**

That the   respondent   may be ordered to pay the costs of this suit if defended.

(3) **Ancillary relief**

That the petitioner may be granted the following ancillary relief:

(a) an order for maintenance pending suit

a periodical payments order

a secured provision order

a lump sum order

a property adjustment order

an order under section 24B, 25B or 25C of the Act of 1973 (Pension Sharing/Attachment Order)

(b) ~~For the children~~

~~a periodical payments order~~

~~a secured provision order~~

~~a lump sum order~~

~~a property adjustment order~~

Signed   *David Brown*

The names and addresses of the persons to be served with the petition are:

Respondent: Jane Brown
Flat 51, Belvedere Drive, Sheffield

Co-Respondent (adultery case only):

The Petitioner's address for service is: David Brown
"Cosy Nook", Doncaster, South Yorkshire

Dated this   16th   day of   September   20 04

Address all communications for the court to: The Court Manager, County Court,

The Court   }
office at   }   Doncaster

is open from 10 a.m. to 4 p.m. (4.30 p.m. at the Principal Registry of the Family Division) on Mondays to Fridays.

Completed example of Form D8 Divorce Petition (Five-Year Separation)
(continued)

In the

Doncaster   County Court*

No.

~~In the Principal Registry*~~

Between   David Brown

Petitioner

and   Jane Brown

Respondent

Divorce Petition

Full name and address of the petitioner or
of solicitors if they are acting for the petitioner.

David Brown
"Cosy Nook"
Doncaster
South Yorkshire

Statement of Arrangements for Children

In the	Croydon	County Court
Petitioner	Susan Smith	
Respondent	James Smith	

	No. of matter *(always quote this)*	93D 0423

To the Petitioner

You must complete this form
If you or the respondent have any children • under 16

or • over 16 but under 18 if they are at school or college or are training for a trade, profession or vocation.

Please use black ink.
Please complete Parts I, II and III.

Before you issue a petition for divorce try to reach agreement with your husband/wife over the proposals for the children's future. There is space for him/her to sign at the end of this form if agreement is reached.

If your husband/wife does not agree with the proposals he/she will have an opportunity at a later stage to state why he/she does not agree and will be able to make his/her own proposals.

You should take or send the completed form, signed by you (and, if agreement is reached, by your husband/wife) together with a copy to the court when you issue your petition.

Please refer to the explanatory notes issued regarding completion of the prayer of the petition if you are asking the court to make any order regarding the children.

The Court will only make an order if it considers that an order will be better for the child(ren) than no order.

If you wish to apply for any of the orders which may be available to you under Part I or II of the Children Act 1989 you are advised to see a solicitor.

You should obtain legal advice from a solicitor or, alternatively, from an advice agency. Addresses of solicitors and advice agencies can be obtained from the Yellow Pages and the Solicitors Regional Directory which can be found at Citizens Advice Bureaux, Law Centres and any local library.

To the Respondent

The petitioner has completed Part I, II and III of this form
which will be sent to the Court at the same time that the divorce petition is filed.

Please read all parts of the form carefully.

If you agree with the arrangements and proposals for the children you should sign Part IV of the form.
Please use black ink. You should return the form to the petitioner, or his/her solicitor.

If you do not agree with all or some of the arrangements of proposals you will be given the opportunity of saying so when the divorce petition is served on you.

D8A - w3 F.P. Rule 2.2(2) (Form M4)(5.95)   1

Completed example of Form D8A Statement of Arrangements for Children (continued)

Part 1 - Details of the children

Please read the instructions for boxes 1, 2 and 3 before you complete this section

---

1. **Children of both parties** *(Give details only of any children born to you and the Respondent or adopted by you both)*

	Forenames	Surname	Date of birth
(i)	Samantha	Smith	14-05-2001
(ii)			
(iii)			
(iv)			
(v)			

---

2. **Other children of the family** *(Give details of any other children treated by both of you as children of the family: for example your own or the Respondent's)*

	Forenames	Surname	Date of birth	Relationship to Yourself	Respondent
(i)	N/A				
(ii)					
(iii)					
(iv)					
(v)					

---

3. **Other children who are not children of the family** *(Give details of any children born to you or the Respondent that have not been treated as children of the family or adopted by you both)*

	Forenames	Surname	Date of birth
(i)	N/A		
(ii)			
(iii)			
(iv)			
(v)			

2

Part II - Arrangements for the children of the family

This part of the form must be completed. Give details for each child if arrangements are different.
(if necessary, continue on another sheet and attach it to this form)

4. **Home details**   *(please tick the appropriate boxes)*

(a) The addresses at which the children now live

The Mill House
Croydon
Surrey

(b) Give details of the number of living rooms, bedrooms, etc. at the addresses in (a)

1 living room
3 bedrooms
1 kitchen
1 bathroom
1 dining room
1 downstairs W.C.

(c) Is the house rented or owned and by whom?

Jointly owned by petitioner and respondent

Is the rent or any mortgage being regularly paid?

☐ No   ✓ Yes

(d) Give the names of all other persons living with the children including your husband/wife if he/she lives there. State their relationship to the children.

James Smith - father

Maria Perez - au pair

(e) Will there be any change in these arrangements?

☐ No   ✓ Yes   *(please give details)*

This house is to be sold

3

Completed example of Form D8A Statement of Arrangements for Children (continued)

5.	**Education and training details**	*(please tick the appropriate boxes)*

(a) Give the names of the school, college or place of training attended by each child.

N/A

(b) Do the children have any special educational needs?

[✓] No   [ ] Yes   *(please give details)*

(c) Is the school, college or place of training, fee-paying?

[ ] No   [ ] Yes   *(please give details of how much the fees are per term / year)*

N/A

Are fees being regularly paid?

[ ] No   [ ] Yes   *(please give details)*

N/A

(d) Will there be any change in these arrangements?

[ ] No   [✓] Yes   *(please give details)*

Samantha has a place at St. Mary's Primary School for September 2006

4

6. **Childcare details** *(please tick the appropriate boxes)*

(a) Which parent looks after the children from day to day? If responsibility is shared, please give details

Mother and au pair

(b) Does that parent go out to work?

[ ] No   [✓] Yes   *(please give details of his/her hour of work)*

Secretary 9:00 - 5:00

(c) Does someone look after the children when the parent is not there?

[ ] No   [✓] Yes   *(please give details)*

Au pair

(d) Who looks after the children during school holidays?

Au pair

(e) Will there be any change in these arrangements?

[✓] No   [ ] Yes   *(please give details)*

7. **Maintenance** *(please tick the appropriate boxes)*

(a) Does your husband/wife pay towards the upkeep of the children? If there is another source of maintenance, please specify.

[ ] No   [✓] Yes   *(please give details of how much)*

£400 per month

(b) Is the payment made under a court order?

[✓] No   [ ] Yes   *(please give details, including the name of the court and the case number)*

(c) Is the payment following an assessment by the Child Support Agency?

[✓] No   [ ] Yes   *(please give details of how much)*

(d) Has maintenance for the children been agreed?

[ ] No   [✓] Yes

(e) If not, will you be applying for: N/A
• a child maintenance order from the court

[ ] No   [ ] Yes

• child support maintenance through the Child Support Agency?

[ ] No   [ ] Yes

8. **Details for contact with the children** *(please tick the appropriate boxes)*

(a) Do the children see your husband/wife?

[ ] No [✓] Yes *(please give details of how often and where)*

We are still living together

(b) Do the children ever stay with your husband/wife?

[ ] No [ ] Yes *(please give details of how much)*

N/A

(c) Will there be any change to these arrangements?

[ ] No [✓] Yes *(please give details of how much)*

The respondent is purchasing a flat for himself on completion of the sale of Mill House. Samantha will have her own room there and spend one night a week and alternate weekends Friday 8 p.m. to Sunday 6 p.m. with the respondent.

Please give details of the proposed arrangements for contact and residence.

6

9. **Details of health**   *(please tick the appropriate boxes)*

(a) Are the children generally in good health?   ☐ No   ☑ Yes   *(please give details of any serious disability or chronic illness)*

(b) Do the children have any special health needs?   ☑ No   ☐ Yes   *(please give details of the care needed and how it is to be provided)*

10. **Details of Care and other court proceedings**   *(please tick the appropriate boxes)*

(a) Are the children in the care of a local authority, or under the supervision of a social worker or probation officer?   ☑ No   ☐ Yes   *(please give details including any court proceedings)*

(b) Are any of the children on the Child Protection Register?   ☑ No   ☐ Yes   *(please give details of the local authority and the date of registration)*

(c) Are there or have there been any proceedings in any court involving the children, for example adoption, custody/residence, access/contact, wardship, care, supervision or maintenance?   ☑ No   ☐ Yes   *(please give details and send a copy of any order to the court)*

(You need not include any Child Support Agency proceedings here)

7

Completed example of Form D8A Statement of Arrangements for Children (continued)

┌─ **Part III   To the Petitioner** ─────────────────────────

Conciliation

If you and your husband/wife do not agree about arrangements for the child(ren), would you agree to discuss the matter with a Conciliator and your husband/wife?   ☐ No   ☑ Yes

Declaration

I declare that the information I have given is correct and complete to the best of my knowledge.

Signed *Susan Smith* . . . . (Petitioner)

Date: . . . 1st July 2004

┌─ **Part IV   To the Respondent** ─────────────────────────

I agree with the arrangements and proposals contained in Part I and II of this form.

Signed . . . *James Smith* . . . . (Respondent)

Date: . . . 5th July 2004

Affidavit by petitioner in support of petition under
Section 1(2)(a) of Matrimonial Causes Act 1973

Family Proceedings
Rule 2.24(3)(Form M7)

No. of Matter   92D 451

In the   Richmond   **County Court***

*Delete as
appropriate*

[Principal Registry of the Family Division*]

Between	Claire Green	(Petitioner)
and	Michael Green	(Respondent)
and		(Co-Respondent)

Question	Answer
About the Divorce Petition	
1. Have you read the petition in this case?	Yes
2. Do you wish to alter or add to any statement in the petition? If so, state the alterations or additions.	No
3. Subject to these alterations or additions (if any) is everything stated **in your petition** true? If any statement is not within your own knowledge, indicate this and say whether it is true to the best of your information and belief.	Yes
4. State briefly your reasons for saying that the respondent has committed the adultery alleged.	The respondent has moved in with another woman.
5. On what date did it first become known to you that the respondent had committed the adultery alleged?	14th May 2004 - The respondent told me that he had committed the adultery alleged.

D80A (12.03)

Printed on behalf of The Court Service

6.	Do you find it intolerable to live with the respondent?	Yes
7.	Since the date given in the answer to Question 5, have you ever lived with the respondent in the same household? If so, state the address and the period (or periods), giving dates.	No

About the children of the family

8.	Have you read the Statement of Arrangements filed in this case?	Yes
9.	Do you wish to alter anything in the Statement of Arrangements or add to it? If so, state the alterations or additions.	No
10.	Subject to these alterations and additions (if any) is everything stated in the **Statement of Arrangements** true? If any statement is not within your own knowledge, indicate this and say whether it is true and correct to the best of your information and belief.	Yes

I,   Claire Green   (full name)

of   1 Apple Cottage, Barnes, London, SW13   (full residential address)

Doctor

(occupation)

make oath and say as follows:-

1.   I am the petitioner in this cause.

2.   **The answers to Questions 1 to 10 above are true.**

(1) Delete if the acknowledgment is signed by a solicitor.

3.(1)   I identify the signature .... Michael Green ....(2)
appearing on the copy acknowledgment of service now produced to me and marked "A" as the signature of my husband/wife, the respondent in this cause.

(2) Insert name of the respondent exactly as it appears on the acknowledgment of service signed by him or her.

~~4.(3)~~ ~~I identify the signature~~ ....(2)
~~appearing at the foot of the document now produced to me and marked "B" as the~~ ~~signature of the respondent.~~

(3) Insert where confession exhibited.

(4)
~~5.~~   I identify the signature .... Michael Green ....(2)
appearing at Part IV of the Statement of Arrangements dated ..... 5th July 2004 ....
now produced to me and marked "C" as the signature of the respondent.

(4) Exhibit any document on which the petitioner wishes to rely.

~~6.(4)~~

(5) If the petitioner seeks a judicial separation, amend accordingly.

(5)
~~7.~~   I ask the court to grant a decree dissolving my marriage with the respondent(5) on the ground stated in my petition [and to order the respondent/co-respondent to pay the costs of this suit](6).

(6) Amend or delete as appropriate.

Sworn at   Richmond   )

in the County of   Surrey   )

this   13th   day of   August   , 2004) .... *Claire Green* ....

Before me, ... *Paul Hammond* ....

(7) Delete as the case may be.

A Commissioner for Oaths
~~Officer of the Court appointed by~~ ~~the Judge to take Affidavits.~~(7)

Completed example of Form D80 Affidavit of Evidence (Adultery) (continued)

No. of Matter   92D 451

In the   Richmond   County Court*

[Principal Registry of the Family Division]*

Between   Claire Green

(Petitioner)

and   Michael Green

(Respondent)

Affidavit by Petitioner in support of petition

under Section 1(2)(a) of

the Matrimonial Causes Act 1973

Solicitors for the Petitioner

Completed example of Form D80 Affidavit of Evidence (Unreasonable Behaviour)

Affidavit by petitioner in support of petition under
Section 1(2)(b) of Matrimonial Causes Act 1973

Family Proceedings
Rule 2.24(3)(Form M7)

No. of Matter   10A 123

In the   Richmond   **County Court***

*Delete as appropriate

[~~Principal Registry of the Family Division*~~]

Between   Susan Smith   (Petitioner)

and   James Smith   (Respondent)

Question	Answer
About the Divorce Petition	
1. Have you read the petition in this case including what is said about the behaviour of the respondent?	Yes
2. Do you wish to alter or add to any statement in the petition or the particulars? If so, state the alterations or additions.	No
3. Subject to these alterations or additions (if any) is everything stated **in your petition and the particulars** true? If any statement is not within your own knowledge, indicate this and say whether it is true to the best of your information and belief.	Yes
4. If you consider that the respondent's behaviour has affected your health, state the effect it has had.	The respondent has committed unreasonable behaviour - being verbally abusive - which has resulted in the petitioner suffering from severe weight loss and depression.

D80B (12.03)   *Printed on behalf of The Court Service*

5. (i) Is the respondent's behaviour as set out in your petition and particulars continuing?	No
ii) If the respondent's behaviour **is not continuing**, what was the date of the final incident relied upon by you in your petition?	1st January 2004 - After a huge bout of verbal abuse, I decided to leave the family home.
6. (i) Since the date given in answer to question 5 or, if no date is given in answer to that question, since the date of the petition, have you lived at the same address as the respondent for a period of more than 6 months, or for periods which together amount to more than 6 months?	No
ii) If so, state the address and the period (or periods), giving dates to the best of your knowledge or belief, and describe the arrangements for sharing the accommodation, including: • whether you have shared a bedroom; • whether you have taken your meals together; • what arrangements you have made for cleaning the accommodation and for other domestic tasks; • what arrangements you have made for the payment of household bills and other expenses.	N/A
About the children of the family	
7. Have you read the Statement of Arrangements filed in this case?	N/A
8. Do you wish to alter anything in the Statement of Arrangements or add to it? If so, state the alterations or additions.	N/A
9. Subject to these alterations and additions (if any) is everything stated in the **Statement of Arrangements** true? If any statement is not within your own knowledge, indicate this and say whether it is true and correct to the best of your information and belief.	N/A

I,   Susan Smith   (full name)

of   1 Meadow Avenue, Bermondsey, SE1   (full residential address)

        Teacher

                                                                              (occupation)

make oath and say as follows:-

(1) Delete if the acknowledgment is signed by a solicitor.

1.   I am the petitioner in this cause.

2.   **The answers to Questions 1 to 9 above are true.**

(2) Insert name of the respondent exactly as it appears on the acknowledgment of service signed by him or her.

3.(1) I identify the signature .....James Smith...(2)
       appearing on the copy acknowledgment of service now produced to me and marked "A"
       as the signature of my husband/wife, the respondent in this cause.

(3) Exhibit any medical report or document on which the petitioner wishes to rely.

4.   I exhibit marked "B" a certificate/report of Dr. ....(3)

5.   I identify the signature ....(2)
      appearing at Part IV of the Statement of Arrangements dated ....
      now produced to me and marked "C" as the signature of the respondent.

(4)

(4) If the petitioner seeks a judicial separation, amend accordingly.

6.   I ask the court to grant a decree dissolving my marriage with the respondent(4) on the
      ground stated in my petition [and to order the respondent to pay the costs of this suit](5).

(5) Amend or delete as appropriate.

Sworn at   Holborn   )
)
in the County of   Greater London   )
)
this   13th day of August   , 2004}   ....*Susan Smith*...................

                                     Before me, ...*Paul Hammond*..................

(6) Delete as the case may be.

A Commissioner for Oaths
Officer of the Court appointed by
the Judge to take Affidavits.(6)

No. of Matter   10A 123

In the   Holborn   County Court*

[Principal Registry of the Family Division]*

Between   Susan Smith

(Petitioner)

and   James Smith

(Respondent)

Affidavit by Petitioner in support of petition

under Section 1(2)(b) of

the Matrimonial Causes Act 1973

Solicitors for the Petitioner

Affidavit by petitioner in support of petition under
Section 1(2)(c) of Matrimonial Causes Act 1973

Family Proceedings
Rule 2.24(3)(Form M7)

No. of Matter   99Z 999

In the   Richmond   **County Court***

*Delete as appropriate

[~~Principal Registry of the Family Division*~~]

Between   David Brown   (Petitioner)

and   Jane Brown   (Respondent)

Question	Answer
About the Divorce Petition	
1. Have you read the petition filed in this case?	Yes
2. Do you wish to alter or add to any statement in the petition or the particulars? If so, state the alterations or additions.	No
3. Subject to these alterations or additions (if any) is everything stated **in your petition** true? If any statement is not within your own knowledge, indicate this and say whether it is true to the best of your information and belief.	Yes
4. State the date on which you and the respondent separated, and, if different, the date on which the alleged desertion began. Did you agree to the separation?	1st January 2001 No
5. State briefly the facts you rely on in support of the allegation that the respondent deserted you, and your reason for saying that the desertion continued up to the presentation of the petition.	The respondent did not tell me that she was leaving. She has not contacted me since 1st January 2001 and has shown no intention to return.
6. Did the respondent ever offer to resume cohabitation?	No

D80C (12.03)   *Printed on behalf of The Court Service*

7. State as far as you know the various addresses at which you and the respondent have respectively lived since the last date given in the answer to Question 4, and the periods of residence at each address.

	Petitioner's Address		Respondent's Address
From		From	
to		to	
1st January 2001 to date	'Seaview', Bournemouth Road, Poole, Dorset	1st January 2001 to date	Flat 5, River Drive, Poole, Dorset

8. Since the last date given in the answer to Question 4, have you ever lived with the respondent in the same household?

   If so, state the address and the period (or periods), giving dates.

   No

About the children of the family

9. Have you read the Statement of Arrangements filed in this case?

   Yes

10. Do you wish to alter anything in the Statement of Arrangements or add to it?

    If so, state the alterations or additions.

    No

11. Subject to these alterations and additions (if any) is everything stated in the **Statement of Arrangements** true?

    If any statement is not within your own knowledge, indicate this and say whether it is true and correct to the best of your information and belief.

    Yes

I,   David Brown   (full name)

of   'Seaview', Bournemouth Road, Poole   (full residential address)

Butcher   (occupation)

make oath and say as follows:-

1.   I am the petitioner in this cause.

2.   **The answers to Questions 1 to 11 above are true.**

(1) Delete if the acknowledgment is signed by a solicitor.

3.[1]   I identify the signature .... Jane Brown ....[2]
appearing on the copy acknowledgment of service now produced to me and marked "A" as the signature of my husband/wife, the respondent in this cause.

(2) Insert name of the respondent exactly as it appears on the acknowledgment of service signed by him or her.

4.[3]   I identify the signature .... Jane Brown ....[2]
appearing at Part IV of the Statement of Arrangements dated ...... 5th July 2004 ......
now produced to me and marked "B" as the signature of the respondent.

(3) Exhibit any other document on which the petitioner wishes to rely.

~~5.~~[3]

(4) If the petitioner seeks a judicial separation, amend accordingly.

(5) Amend or delete as appropriate.

(5)
~~6.~~   I ask the court to grant a decree dissolving my marriage with the respondent[4] on the ground stated in my petition [~~and to order the respondent to pay the costs of this suit~~][5].

Sworn at   Poole   )

in the County of   Dorset   )

this   13th   day of   August   , 2004) ...... *David Brown* ......

Before me, ... *Paul Hammond* ......

(6) Delete as the case may be.

~~A Commissioner for Oaths~~
Officer of the Court appointed by the Judge to take Affidavits.[6]

No. of Matter   99Z 999

In the   Poole   County Court*

[Principal Registry of the Family Division]*

Between   David Brown

(Petitioner)

and   Jane Brown

(Respondent)

Affidavit by Petitioner in support of petition

under Section 1(2)(c) of

the Matrimonial Causes Act 1973

Solicitors for the Petitioner

Completed example of Form D80 Affidavit of Evidence (Two-Year Separation)

Affidavit by petitioner in support of petition under
Section 1(2)(d) of Matrimonial Causes Act 1973

Family Proceedings
Rule 2.24(3)(Form M7)

No. of Matter   44B 971

In the   Essex   **County Court***

*Delete as appropriate

[Principal Registry of the Family Division*]

Between   Trevor Harding   (Petitioner)

and   Patricia Harding   (Respondent)

Question	Answer
About the Divorce Petition	
1. Have you read the petition filed in this case?	Yes
2. Do you wish to alter or add to any statement in the petition or the particulars? If so, state the alterations or additions.	No
3. Subject to these alteration or additions (if any), is everything stated **in your petition** true? If any statement is not within your own knowledge, indicate this and say whether it is true to the best of your information and belief.	Yes
4. State the date on which you and the respondent separated.	1st July 2002
5. State briefly the reason or main reason for the separation.	We have grown apart and had no common interests.
6. State the date when, and the circumstances in which, you came to the conclusion that the marriage was in fact at an end.	10th April 2002 when the respondent asked for a separation.

D80D (12.03)   *Printed on behalf of The Court Service*

7. State as far as you know the various addresses at which you and the respondent have respectively lived since the last date given in the answer to Question 4, and the periods of residence at each address.

	Petitioner's Address		Respondent's Address
From		From	
to		to	
1st July 2002 to date	14 Rose Way, Colchester, Essex	1st July 2002 to date	93B Daisy Crescent, Manchester

8. Since the date given in the answer to Question 4, have you ever lived with the respondent in the same household?

   If so, state the address and the period (or periods), giving dates.

   No

About the children of the family

9. Have you read the Statement of Arrangements filed in this case?

   Yes

10. Do you wish to alter anything in the Statement of Arrangements or add to it?

    If so, state the alterations or additions.

    No

11. Subject to these alterations and additions (if any) is everything stated in the **Statement of Arrangements** true?

    If any statement is not within your own knowledge, indicate this and say whether it is true and correct to the best of your information and belief.

    Yes

I,   Trevor Harding   (full name)

of   14 Rose Way, Colchester, Essex   (full residential address)

      Grocer   (occupation)

make oath and say as follows:-

1.   I am the petitioner in this cause.

2.   **The answers to Questions 1 to 11 above are true.**

(1) Delete if the acknowledgment is signed by a solicitor.

(2) Insert name of the respondent exactly as it appears on the acknowledgment of service signed by him or her.

3.(1)   I identify the signature ...... Patricia Harding ....(2)
appearing on the copy acknowledgment of service now produced to me and marked "A" as the signature of my husband/wife, the respondent in this cause.

(3) Exhibit any other document on which the petitioner wishes to rely.

4.(3)   I identify the signature ...... Patricia Harding ....(2)
appearing at Part IV of the Statement of Arrangements dated .... 5th July 2004 ....
now produced to me and marked "B" as the signature of the respondent.

~~5.~~(3)

(4) If the petitioner seeks a judicial separation, amend accordingly.

(5) Amend or delete as appropriate.

(5)

~~6.~~   I ask the court to grant a decree dissolving my marriage with the respondent(4) on the ground stated in my petition [~~and to order the respondent to pay the costs of this suit~~](5).

Sworn at   Colchester   )

in the County of   Essex   )

this   13th   day of   August   , 2004) *Trevor Harding*

(6) Delete as the case may be.

Before me,   *Paul Hammond*

A Commissioner for Oaths
~~Officer of the Court appointed by the Judge to take Affidavits.~~(6)

Completed example of Form D80 Affidavit of Evidence (Two-Year Separation) (continued)

No. of Matter   44B 971

In the   Essex   County Court*

[~~Principal Registry of the Family Division~~]*

Between   Trevor Harding

(Petitioner)

and   Patricia Harding

(Respondent)

Affidavit by Petitioner in support of petition

under Section 1(2)(d) of

the Matrimonial Causes Act 1973

Solicitors for the Petitioner

Completed example of Form D80 Affidavit of Evidence (Five-Year Separation)

Affidavit by petitioner in support of petition under
Section 1(2)(e) of Matrimonial Causes Act 1973

Family Proceedings
Rule 2.24(3)(Form M7)

No. of Matter   11A 111

In the   Doncaster   **County Court***

*Delete as
appropriate*   [Principal Registry of the Family Division*]

Between   Fiona Blatch   (Petitioner)

and   Simon Blatch   (Respondent)

Question	Answer
About the Divorce Petition	
1. Have you read the petition filed in this case?	Yes
2. Do you wish to alter or add to any statement in the petition or the particulars? If so, state the alterations or additions.	No
3. Subject to these alterations or additions (if any) is everything stated **in your petition** true? If any statement is not within your own knowledge, indicate this and say whether it is true to the best of your information and belief.	Yes
4. State the date on which you and the respondent separated.	1st January 1999
5. State briefly the reason or main reason for the separation.	The respondent wanted a new life.
6. State the date when and the circumstances in which you came to the conclusion that the marriage was in fact at an end.	Christmas 1998 when the respondent told me he was leaving me.

D80E (12.03)   *Printed on behalf of The Court Service*

7. State as far as you know the various addresses at which you and the respondent have respectively lived since the last date given in the answer to Question 4, and the periods of residence at each address.

	Petitioner's Address		Respondent's Address
From		From	
to		to	
1st January 1999 to date	'Cosy Nook', Doncaster, South Yorkshire	1st January 1999 to date	Flat 51, Belvedere Drive, Sheffield

8. Since the last date given in the answer to Question 4, have you ever lived with the respondent in the same household?

   If so, state the address and the period (or periods), giving dates.

   No

About the children of the family

9. Have you read the Statement of Arrangements filed in this case?

   N/A

10. Do you wish to alter anything in the Statement of Arrangements or add to it?

    If so, state the alterations or additions.

    N/A

11. Subject to these alterations and additions (if any) is everything stated in the **Statement of Arrangements** true?

    If any statement is not within your own knowledge, indicate this and say whether it is true and correct to the best of your information and belief.

    N/A

I,   Fiona Blatch   (full name)

of   'Cosy Nook', Doncaster, South Yorkshire   (full residential address)

      Shop Assistant   (occupation)

make oath and say as follows:-

1.   I am the petitioner in this cause.

2.   **The answers to Questions 1 to 11 above are true.**

(1) Delete if the acknowledgment is signed by a solicitor.

3.(1)   I identify the signature ...... Simon Blatch ....(2) appearing on the copy acknowledgment of service now produced to me and marked "A" as the signature of my husband/wife, the respondent in this cause.

(2) Insert name of the respondent exactly as it appears on the acknowledgment of service signed by him or her.

4.(3) ~~I identify the signature~~ ....(2) ~~appearing at Part IV of the Statement of Arrangements dated~~ .... ~~now produced to me and marked "B" as the signature of the respondent.~~

(3) Exhibit any other document on which the petitioner wishes to rely.

5.(3)

(4) If the petitioner seeks a judicial separation, amend accordingly.

(4)

6.~~.~~   I ask the court to grant a decree dissolving my marriage with the respondent(4) on the ground stated in my petition [and to order the respondent to pay the costs of this suit](5).

(5) Amend or delete as appropriate.

Sworn at   Doncaster   )
)
in the County of South Yorkshire   )
)
this   13th day of August   , 2004)   *Fiona Blatch*
....

Before me, *Paul Hammond* ....

A Commissioner for Oaths
~~Officer of the Court appointed by the Judge to take Affidavits.~~ (6)

(6) Delete as the case may be.

No. of Matter   11A 111

In the   Doncaster   County Court*

[Principal Registry of the Family Division]*

Between   Fiona Blatch

(Petitioner)

and   Simon Blatch

(Respondent)

Affidavit by Petitioner in support of petition

under Section 1(2)(e) of

the Matrimonial Causes Act 1973

Solicitors for the Petitioner

In the   Doncaster   **County Court**

No of matter   92D 451

Between	Carol Moore	Petitioner
and	Geoffrey Moore	Respondent
~~and~~		~~Co-respondent~~

F.P.Rules 2.24

Application for directions for trial (Special Procedure)

The petitioner   Carol Moore

applies to the District Judge for directions for the trial of this undefended cause by entering it in the Special Procedure List.

The petitioner's affidivit of evidence is lodged with this application.

Signed   *Carol Moore*   [~~Solicitor for~~] the petitioner

Dated   1st July 2004

If you write to the Court please address your letters to "The Court Manager" and quote the **No. of the matter** at the top of this form.

The Court Office is at   74 Waterdale, Doncaster, South Yorkshire, DN1 3BT

and is open from 10am to 4pm on Monday to Friday.

D84

Completed example of Form D36 Notice of Application for Decree Nisi to be Made Absolute

---

In the   Doncaster   **County Court**

No. of matter:

Between	Carol Moore	Petitioner
And	Geoffrey Moore	Respondent
~~And~~		~~Co-Respondent~~

Seal

TAKE NOTICE that the Petitioner   Carol Moore

applies for the decree nisi pronounced in his (her) favour

on the 20th day of   June   [2004], to be made absolute.

Dated   7th August 2004

Signed   *Carol Moore*
~~Solicitors for~~ Petitioner

To the Court Manager.

Address all communications to the Court Manager AND QUOTE THE ABOVE CASE NUMBER.

The Court Office at   **74 Waterdale, Doncaster, South Yorkshire, DN1 3BT**

is open from 10a.m. to 4p.m. Monday to Friday.

Notice of Application for Decree Nisi to be made Absolute.
MATRIMONIAL CAUSES RULES - Rule 65(1)

Printed on behalf of the Court Service   **D36** (12.98)

FINANCIAL

STATEMENT

*Applicant/*Respondent

In the

*[County Court]
*[Principal Registry of the Family Division]

*(delete as appropriate)

Between   Applicant   and   Respondent

Solicitor's Ref: Solicitor's Ref:

Please fill in this form fully and accurately. Where any box is not applicable write "N/A". You have a duty to the court to give a full, frank and clear disclosure of all your financial and other relevant circumstances.

A failure to give full and accurate disclosure may result in any order the court makes being set aside.

If you are found to have been deliberately untruthful, criminal proceedings for perjury may be taken against you.

You must attach documents to the form where they are specifically sought and you may attach other documents where it is necessary to explain or clarify any of the information that you give.

Essential documents, which **must** accompany this Statement, are detailed at questions 2.1, 2.2, 2.3, 2.5, 2.14, 2.18 and 2.20.

If there is not enough room on the form for any particular piece of information, you may continue on an attached sheet of paper.

This statement must be sworn before an Officer of the Court,
a solicitor or a Commissioner for Oaths
before it is filed with the Court
or sent to the other party
(see page 20).

Form E Financial Statement (12.00)   *Printed on behalf of The Court Service*   1

Blank example of Form E Financial Statement (continued)

Part 1 General Information

1.1 Full Name

| **1.2 Date of Birth** | Date | Month | Year | **1.3 Date of Marriage** | Date | Month | Year |

1.4 Occupation

| **1.5 Date of the separation** | Date | Month | Year | Tick here | if not applicable |

1.6 Date of the:

	Petition			**Decree Nisi/Decree of Judicial Separation**			**Decree Absolute**		
	Date	Month	Year	Date	Month	Year	Date	Month	Year

| **1.7 If you have remarried, or will remarry, state the date** | Date | Month | Year |

1.8 Do you live with another person?   Yes   No

1.9 Do you intend to live with someone within the next six months?   Yes   No

1.10 Details of any children of the family	Full names	Date of Birth			With whom does the child live?
		Date	Month	Year	

1.11 Give details of the state of health of yourself and the children

Yourself	Children

2

1.12 Give details of the present and proposed future educational arrangements for the children.

Present arrangements	Future arrangements

1.13 Give details of any Child Support Maintenance Assessments or Child Maintenance Orders made between the parties. If no assessment or agreement has been made, give an estimate of the liability of the non-residential parent under the Child Support Act 1991, in respect of the children of the family.

1.14 If this application is to vary an order, give details of the order that is to be varied and attach a copy of the order. Give the reasons for asking for the order to be varied.

1.15 Give details of any other court cases between you and your husband/wife, whether in relation to money, property, children or anything else.

Case No	Court

1.16 Specify your present residence and the occupants of it and on what terms you occupy it (e.g. tenant, owner-occupier).

Address	Occupants	Terms of occupation

3

Blank example of Form E Financial Statement (continued)

Part 2 Financial Details *Capital: Realisable Assets*

*If you have obtained a valuation within the last six months attach a copy. If not, give your own estimate of the property value. A copy of your most recent mortgage statement is also required.

2.1 Give details of your interest in the matrimonial home.

Property name and address	Land Registry Title No.	Nature and extent of your interest	*Property value

Mortgagee's name and address	Type of mortgage	Balance outstanding on any mortgage	Total current value of your beneficial interest
1.			
2.			
Other:			

NET value of your interest in the matrimonial home (A)

2.2 Give details of all other properties, land and buildings in which you have an interest.

Property name(s) and address(es)	Land Registry Title No.	Nature and extent of your interest	*Property value
1.			
2.			
3.			

Mortgagee's Name(s) and address(es)	Type of mortgage	Balance outstanding on any mortgage	Total current value of your interest
1.			
2.			
3.			

TOTAL value of the above (B1)
(not including the matrimonial home)

4

2.3 Give details of all bank, building society and National Savings accounts, in credit, which you hold or have an interest in. Include all PEPs, TESSAs and ISAs. For joint accounts, give your interest and the name of the account holder. If the account is overdrawn, include in Liabilities section at 2.12. *You must attach your bank statements covering the last 12 months for each account listed.*

Name of bank or building society, including branch name	Type of account (e.g. current)	Account number	Name of other account holder (if applicable)	Balance at the date of this statement	Total current value of your interest
1.					
2.					
3.					
4.					
5.					

TOTAL value of your interest in ALL accounts (B2)

2.4 Give details of all stocks, gilts and other quoted securities which you hold or have an interest in. Do not include dividend income as this will be dealt with separately later on.

Name	Type	Size	Current value	Total current value of your interest

TOTAL value of your interest in ALL holdings (B3)

2.5 Give details of all life insurance policies which you hold or in which you have an interest, including those that do not have a surrender value, for each policy.

Policy details, including name of company, policy type and number	If policy is charged, state in whose favour and amount of charge	Maturity date			Surrender value	Total current value of your interest
		Date	Month	Year		

You must attach any surrender value quotations **TOTAL value of your interest in ALL policies** (B4)

5

2.6 Give details of all issues of National Savings Certificates which you hold or have an interest in.

Name of issue	Nominal amount	Current value	Total current value of your interest

TOTAL value of ALL your certificates   (B5)

2.7 Give details of all National Savings Bonds (including Premium Bonds) and other bonds which you hold or have an interest in.

Type of Bond	Bond-holder's number	Current value	Total current value of your interest

(B6)

TOTAL value of ALL your bonds

2.8 Give details of all monies which are OWED TO YOU. Include sums owed in director's or partnership accounts.

Brief description of debt	Balance outstanding	Total current value of your interest

TOTAL value of your interest in ALL debts owed to you   (B7)

2.9 Give details of all cash savings held in excess of £300. You must state where it is held and the currency it is held in.

Where held	Amount	Currency	Total current value of your interest

TOTAL value of ALL your cash (B8)

2.10 Give details of personal belongings individually worth more than £500.
Include cars (gross value), collections, pictures, jewellery, furniture and household belongings (this list is not exhaustive).

Item	Sale value	Total estimated current value of your interest

TOTAL value of your interest in ALL personal belongings (B9)

2.11 Give details of any other realisable assets not yet mentioned, for example, unit trusts, investment trusts, commodities, business expansion schemes and futures (this list is not exhaustive). This is where you must mention any other realisable assets.

Type	Current value	Total current value of your interest

TOTAL value of your interest in ALL other realisable assets (B10)

Now add together all the figures in the previous total boxes (B1 to B10) to give the TOTAL current value of ALL your interest in realisable assets.   **(B)**

7

Part 2 Financial Details   *Capital: Liabilities*

2.12 Give details of any liabilities you have. Exclude mortgages on property dealt with above.
Include money owed on credit cards and store cards, bank loans, hire purchase agreements and any
overdrawn bank or building society accounts.

Liability (i.e. total amount owed, current monthly payments and term of loan/debt)	Current amount	Total current value of your share of the liability

TOTAL value of ALL your liabilities   (C1)

Part 2 Financial Details   *Capital: Capital Gains Tax*

**2.13 If any Capital Gains Tax would be payable on the disposal now of any of your realisable assets,
give your estimate of the tax.**

Asset	Capital Gains Tax	Total current value of your liability

TOTAL value of ALL your Capital Gains Tax liabilities   (C2)

Now add together C1 + C2 to give: **(C)**
TOTAL net value of your liabilities

Now take the liabilities total from the realisable
assets total (A+B-C), to give: **(D)**
TOTAL net value of your personal assets

8

Part 2 Financial Details   *Capital: Business Assets*

2.14 Give details of all your business interests.

You must attach a copy of the last 2 years, accounts and any other document on which you base your valuation.

Name and nature of your business	Your ESTIMATE of the current value of your interest	Your ESTIMATE of any possible Capital Gains Tax payable on disposal	Basis of valuation *(No formal valuation is required at this time)*	What is the extent of your interest?	Total net current value of your interest

TOTAL current value of your interest in business assets   (E)

2.15 List any directorships you hold or held in the last 12 months.

Part 2 Financial Details

Capital: Pensions *(including SERPS but excluding Basic State Pensions)*

2.16 Give details of your pension interests.

If you have been provided with a valuation of your pension rights by the trustees or managers of the pension scheme you must attach it. Where the information is not available, give the estimated date when it will be available and attach the letter to the pension company or administrators from whom the information was sought. If you have more than one pension plan or scheme, you must provide the information in respect of each one, continuing, if necessary, on a separate piece of paper. If you have made Additional Voluntary Contributions or any Free Standing Additional Voluntary Contributions to any plan or scheme, you must give the information separately if the benefits referable to such contributions are separately recorded or paid. If you have more than one pension scheme you should reproduce the information for each scheme. Please include any SERPS.

Information about the Scheme(s)

Name and address of scheme, plan or policy

Your National Insurance number

Number of scheme, plan or policy

Type of scheme, plan or policy *(e.g. final salary, money purchase or other)*

CETV - Cash Equivalent Transfer Value

CETV value

The lump sum payable on death in service before retirement

The lump sum payable on death in deferment before retirement

The lump sum payable on death after retirement

Retirement Benefits

Earliest date when benefit can be paid

The estimated lump sum and monthly pension payable on retirement, assuming you take the maximum lump sum

The estimated monthly pension without taking any lump sum

Spouse's Benefit

On death in service

On death in deferment

On death in retirement

Dependant's Benefit

On death in service

On death in deferment

On death in retirement

TOTAL value of your pension assets　　　　　　**(F)**

10

Note: It is advisable to photocopy this part of the form and send it to your pension providers so that they can complete it for you. They have to provide **one** free quote so make sure not to make more than one request.

Part 2 Financial Details *Capital: Other Assets*

2.17 Give details of any other assets not listed above.

Include the following (this list is not exhaustive):

Unrealisable assets.

Share option scheme, stating the estimated net sale proceeds of the shares if the options were capable of exercise now, and whether Capital GainsT ax or IncomeT ax would be payable.

Trust interests (including interests under a discretionary trust), stating your estimate of the value of the interest and when it is likely to become realisable. If you say it will never be realisable, or has no value, give your reasons.

Specify also any asset that is likely to be received in the forseeable future, any assets held on your behalf by a third party and any assets not mentioned elsewhere in this form held outside England and Wales.

Type of Asset	Value	Total net value of your interest

Total value of your other assets   **(G)**

Total value of your net assets (excluding pensions) (D+E+G)   **(H)**

Total value of your net assets (including pension) (H+F)   **(I)**

11

Part 2 Financial Details   *Income*   *You must attach your last three payslips and your P60 for the most recently completed financial year.*

2.18 Earned Income. Give details of your gross and net income in the last financial year, and in the current financial year.

Nature of income (e.g. salary, bonus)	Last financial year		Current financial year *(estimated for the whole year)*	
	Gross	Net	Gross	Net

2.19 Additional Income: benefits etc. Give details and the value of all benefits in kind, perks, or other remuneration not disclosed elsewhere, received in the last financial year and current financial year.

Nature of income	Last financial year	Current financial year *(estimated for the whole year)*

12

Income *continued*

2.20 Self-employed or partnership income. Give details of annual net profit or loss for the last two accounting years, your share of this figure and tax payable to date of the last accounts and the estimate of income since that date. State the date on which your accounting year begins. Year 2 should be the most recent year, Year 1 the previous year. Please state the "from" and "to" dates for the years concerned.

Nature of income and date your accounting year begins	Details of the last two accounting periods					
	Net profit/loss		Your share of profit/loss		Tax payable by you	
	Year 1	Year 2	Year 1	Year 2	Year 1	Year 2

	Net Income	Estimate	
Net income SINCE date of last accounts and estimate for the whole year			*You must attach the accounts for the last two completed accounting years*

2.21 Investment income (e.g. dividends, interest). Give details of net income received in the last financial year, and in the current financial year, and state whether it was paid gross or net of income tax. You are not required to calculate any tax payable that may arise.

Nature of income and the asset from which it derived	Paid gross or net (*delete that which is not applicable*)	Last financial year	Current financial year
	Gross / Net		

2.22 State benefits (including state pension). Give details of all state benefits received in the last 52 weeks.

Nature of income	Total income received in the last 52 weeks

13

2.23 Any other income. Give details of any other income received in the last 52 weeks.

Nature of income	Total income for the last 52 weeks

Part 2 Financial Details   *Summaries*

2.24 Summary of your income.

Your estimate of your current annual net income from all sources (2.18 - 2.23)	Your estimate of your net income from all sources for the next 52 weeks
	£ **(J)**

2.25 Summary of financial information.

	Reference of the section on this statement	Value
Net value of your interest in the matrimonial home	A	
Total current value of all your interest in the other realisable assets	B	
Total net value of your liabilities	C	
Total net value of your personal assets	D	
Total current value of your interest in business assets	E	
Total current value of your pension or transfer values	F	
Total value of your other assets	G	
Total value of your net assets *(excluding pension)*	H	
Total value of your net assets *(including pension)*	I	
Your estimated net income for the next 52 weeks	J	

14

Part 3 Requirements   *Income Needs*

3.1 Give the reasonable future income needs of yourself (e.g. housing, car etc) and of any children living with you, or provided for by you. This may be expressed as annual, monthly or weekly figures (state which), but you should not use a combination of any of these periods.

Item	*Income needs of yourself*	Amount
	sub-total	

Item	*Income needs of child(ren) living with you, or provided for by you.*	Amount
	sub-total	

Total income needs

15

Part 3 Requirements   *Capital Needs*

3.2 Give the reasonable future capital needs of yourself and of any children living with you, or provided for by you.

Item	*Capital needs of yourself*	Cost

sub-total

Item	*Capital needs of child(ren) living with you, or provided for by you.*	Cost

sub-total

Total capital needs

16

Part 4 Other Information

4.1 State whether there has been any significant change in your net assets during the last 12 months, including any assets held outside England and Wales (e.g. closure of any bank or building society accounts).

4.2 Give brief details of the standard of living enjoyed by you and your spouse during the marriage.

4.3 Are there any particular contributions to the family property and assets or outgoings, or to family life, that have been made by you, your partner or anyone else that you think should be taken into account? If so, give a brief description of the contribution, the amount, when it was made, and by whom.

4.4 Bad behaviour or conduct by the other party will only be taken into account in very exceptional circumstances when deciding how the assets should be divided after divorce. If you feel it should be taken into account in your case identify the nature of the behaviour or conduct.

17

Part 4 Other Information *continued*

4.5 Give details of any other circumstances which you consider could significantly affect the extent of the financial provision to be made by or for you or for any child of the family, e.g. earning capacity, disability, inheritance prospects or redundancy, remarriage and cohabitation plans, any contingent liabilities. (This list is not exhaustive.)

4.6 If you have remarried (or intend to) or are living with another person (or intend to), give brief details, so far as they are known to you, of his or her income and assets.

Annual Income		Assets	
Nature of income	Value (state whether gross or net, if known)	Item	Value (if known)
Total		Total	

18

Part 5 Order Sought

5.1 If you are able to at this stage, specify what kind of orders you are asking the court to make, and state whether at this stage you see the case being appropriate for a "clean break". (A "clean break" means a settlement or order which provides, amongst other things, that neither you nor your spouse will have any further claim against the income or capital of the other party. A clean break does not terminate the responsibility of a parent to a child.)

5.2 **If you are seeking a transfer or settlement of any property or other asset, you must identify the asset in question.

5.3 **If you are seeking a variation of a pre-nuptial or post-nuptial settlement, you must identify the settlement, by whom it was made, its trustees and beneficiaries, and state why you allege it is a nuptial settlement.

** Important Note: Where 5.2, 5.3 (above) or 5.4 (overleaf) apply, you should seek legal advice before completing the sections.

19

Blank example of Form E Financial Statement (continued)

Part 5 Order Sought *continued*

5.4 **If you are seeking an avoidance of disposition order, you must identify the property to which the disposition relates and the person or body in whose favour the disposition is alleged to have been made.

I *(the above-named Applicant/Respondent)*

make oath and confirm that the information given above is a full, frank, clear and accurate disclosure of my financial and other relevant circumstances.

of

Signed Dated

Address all communications to the Court Manager of the Court and quote the case number from page 1. If you do not quote this number, your correspondence may be returned.

The court office at
is open from 10a.m. to 4p.m. (4.30p.m. at the Principal Registry of the Family Division) on Monday to Friday only.

20

DATED   200[   ]

(1) **[Name]**

(2) **[Name]**

DEED OF SEPARATION

THIS DEED OF SEPARATION is made the
[   ] day of [   ]
two thousand and [   ]

BETWEEN:

(1)   [Name] of [address] ('the husband')

(2)   [Name] of [address] ('the wife')

WHEREAS:

1.   The husband and the wife were married on
[19   ][20   ] and there [is]/[are] child[ren]
of the [family]/[marriage], namely,
(born   ) [and   (born   )].

2.   The husband and the wife have lived separate
and apart [as separate households at   ]
in circumstances which they agree to be
permanent since   [19   ][20   ]
('the date of separation') [with a view to
their marriage being dissolved].

OR

3.   The husband and the wife have agreed to live
separate and apart permanently from each
other as from   [19   ][20   ] ('the date
of separation') [with a view to their marriage
being dissolved] and that the terms of this
deed shall only take effect from the date of
separation.

**WARNING: PLEASE READ ALL FOOTNOTES
VERY CAREFULLY**

4.   The husband and the wife wish to regulate
the terms of their separation and are entering
into this deed for that purpose; the husband
and the wife acknowledge that they enter into
it without any pressure or duress whatsoever.

5.   The husband and the wife have formally and
frankly disclosed to each other their means
and financial circumstances which are set out
in summary form in Appendix A to this Deed.

6.   **(If appropriate)** The husband has paid to the
wife the sum of £[   ] in full and final
satisfaction of the wife's claims against the
husband and against his Estate as to capital and
income now and upon a divorce between the
husband and the wife **(if the payment made is
to satisfy only the wife's claim for capital and
not her claim for income then the reference to
the wife's claims for income and against the
husband's Estate should be deleted).**

7.   The furniture and all other contents of the
property(ies) at **[please insert address or
addresses here]** have already been divided by
agreement between the husband and the wife.

NOW THIS DEED WITNESSES

8.   **(Will be either)** The husband and the wife
will continue to live separate and apart.

8.   **(or)** The husband and the wife will continue
to live as separate households at **[insert
address]** until such time as one or other
leaves and thereafter they will continue to live
separate and apart.

9.   At the expiration of 2 years from the date of
separation **OR** on or before the [   ] day of
[   ] 200[   ] the wife/husband[1] will issue a
divorce petition at the [   ] county
court on the grounds of **[either the
wife's/husband's unreasonable behaviour OR
two years separation]** in a form to be agreed
by the parties prior to issue. The husband/wife[2]
will consent to the granting of a decree of
divorce in such proceedings, will confirm this
consent as necessary to the Court and will not
withdraw this consent. The wife/husband[3] will
pursue such proceedings with reasonable speed
and will apply for decree nisi to be made
absolute to be made on the earliest possible
date. The costs of these proceedings shall be
born by the husband/wife/wife and husband
in equal shares.

10.   The husband and the wife acknowledge that
the financial arrangements contained in this
Deed are accepted in full and final
satisfaction of all claims which each may be
entitled to make against the other's income
capital or property whosever and wheresoever
arising under the present or future laws.

11.   The husband and the wife invite the court in
the divorce proceedings referred to in clause 9
above to make an order which mirrors exactly
the financial arrangements contained in this
Deed and to dismiss all and any claims which
each may have against the other's financial
provision and property adjustment (save that
where one party is to receive periodical
payments from the other then the recipient's
claims for periodical payments shall not be
dismissed) and to direct that neither party
shall be entitled in relation to this marriage to
make an application under the matrimonial
causes act 1973 section 23 (1) (a) or (b).

12.   The husband and the wife covenant that
neither will make any claim against the estate
of the other and will invite the court in the
divorce proceedings referred to in clause 9
above to make an order pursuant to the
Inheritance (Provision for Family and

[1] *Delete either wife or husband here as appropriate.*
[2] *Retain only the spouse who was deleted in (1).*
[3] *Should be same as in (1).*

Dependants) Act 1975, section 15 that neither of them shall be entitled on the death of the other to apply for an order under section 2 of that Act, save that where one of the parties is in receipt of periodical payments pursuant to this Deed, then that party's ability to make claims of an income nature only against the estate of the other shall not be affected by this clause.

13.   [IF APPROPRIATE] The husband do pay to the wife a lump sum of £[   ] payable within [   ] days of the date of this Deed [or payable by a certain date if that is preferable] and it is agreed that should the payment be made late then interest shall accrue on it until payment at a rate of [   ]% over the [   ] Bank Plc base rate.

14.   [IF APPROPRIATE] The husband will on or before [date] transfer to the wife absolutely all his legal estate and beneficial interest in the property(ies) known as [address] ('the Property(ies)') registered at HM Land Registry under title number [   ] [free of any charge mortgage or any other encumberance/subject to the mortgage in favour of the [   ] Bank/Building Society in respect of which the wife undertakes to use her best endeavours to secure the husband's release and in the meantime to indemnify the husband[4].

15.   [IF APPROPRIATE] The husband and wife agree that the property known as [address] ('the Property') will be sold with vacant possession that the following provisions shall apply in consequence:

15.1   the husband and wife shall agree the estate agents or agents who shall have conduct of the sale and they shall also agree the price at which the property shall be offered for sale, in default of such agreement accepting the recommendations of the selling agent;

15.2   the husband and wife agree to take all necessary steps to co-operate in the marketing and sale of the property, to keep the property in good order pending sale and to execute all documents of sale upon being required to do so and to give vacant possession on the date of completion. Pending sale of the property the husband and the wife shall contribute to all outgoings in relation to the property in the following way:

[please insert arrangements to cover mortgage payments, household bills and other outgoings pending sale];

15.3   neither the husband nor the wife shall further charge the property nor their interest in it, nor lease it nor enter into any other kind of arrangement or agreement in letting the property in writing or made orally without the prior written consent of the other party;

15.4   upon completion of the sale of the property the net proceeds of sale will be divided between the husband and the wife in the following way [insert details of capital division of sale proceeds].

16.   [IF APPROPRIATE] The husband and the wife agree that the policy of life assurance effected with [   ] be assigned to the husband/wife by [date] or within [   ] days of the completion of the sale of the property at clause [   ] above. [IF APPROPRIATE] in consideration of the assignment of this policy the wife/husband shall simultaneously with the assignment pay to the wife/husband the sum of £[   ]. All premiums following the assignment of the policy shall be paid by the wife/husband.[5]

17.   The husband and the wife agree that in the context of the divorce proceedings mentioned at clause 9 above they will, in financial proceedings, seek an order that there be pension sharing orders in relation to the following pensions [insert details of the pensions and also details of what proportion of each fund is to be transferred to the other party.][6]

18.   From the date of this Deed the husband will pay to the wife maintenance in the sum of £[] per annum payable calendar monthly in advance until the first to occur of the following events:

18.1   the death of the wife;

18.2   the death of the husband;

18.3   the wife's remarriage;

18.4   [if appropriate] the cohabitation of the wife for a period or periods in excess of [   ] months;

18.5   a subsequent agreement between the husband and the wife recorded in a supplemental Deed;

[4] *Please note that if the transfer of a property is to be subject to a mortgage then the consent of the mortgage lender will be required. Not also that this deed in itself is not sufficient to transfer title to a property – you must see a conveyancing solicitor to achieve this.*

[5] *Note this deed alone is not sufficient to assign an interest in a policy. You need to obtain a deed of assignment from the insurance company.*

[6] *Legal advice should be obtained regarding pension sharing orders. This deed alone is not sufficient to divide a pension between a couple or to assign any rights in a pension from one spouse to another.*

18.6 a court order varying the terms of this Deed;

18.7 resumption of cohabitation between the husband and the wife for a period of more than [ ] months;

18.8 **[if appropriate]** the [ ] day of [ ] 200[ ].

19. Whilst the children reside primarily with the wife, the husband will pay to the wife from the date of this Deed for the benefit of [each of] the said child[ren] the sum of £[ ] per annum payable calendar monthly in advance in respect of general maintenance [together with such sum as shall equal school fees plus reasonable extras at the schools (selected and agreed by the husband and wife) and attended by the said child[ren] from time to time by way of three payments per annum each made no later than the day before the first day of each school term until the child[ren] shall (respectively) attain the age of 17 years or cease full time secondary education, whichever is the later. This obligation shall come to an end if there shall be any Child Support Agency assessment or any court order providing for financial provision for the child[ren].[7]

20. The assets listed in Annex A shall be retained by the wife as her own property.

21. The assets listed in Annex B shall be retained by the husband as his own property.

22. The husband and the wife shall each retain as their own absolute property all assets not otherwise specifically dealt with by this Deed.

23. The husband and the wife agree that their joint account number [ ] held with [ ] Bank Plc/Building Society shall be closed within [ ] days of the execution of this Deed and the closing balance divided equally between them.

24. The husband and the wife agree not to pledge the credit of the other.

25. The husband and the wife will co-operate in closing all joint credit card accounts and where either holds a card on an account in the name of the other then they shall deliver up that card to the other within [ ] days of the date of this Deed and do everything necessary to terminate such rights as they may have to draw against such credit card accounts and will not attempt to make any expenditure using such credit cards.

26. The husband and the wife agree that it is at present in the best interests of the child[ren]

to have one primary home and that for the time being that home should be with the wife/husband. The husband and the wife also agree that the child[ren] should have contact with the husband/wife and they will agree the arrangements for that contact between them. Any variation of this Deed shall only be effective if recorded by a supplemental Deed executed by both parties.

27. The parties agree that this Deed and its terms shall be governed by the Laws of England and Wales and any part or term of this Deed which is ruled contrary to the Laws of England and Wales shall not invalidate the remainder of this Deed.

IN WITNESS whereof this deed has been executed by the parties hereto and is intended to be and is hereby delivered on the day and year first before written

SIGNED AS A DEED by the said wife

in the presence of

....

....

....

Witness signs and prints full name, and address here

SIGNED AS A DEED by the said husband

in the presence of

....

....

....

Witness signs and prints full name, and address here

---

[7] *This clause does not prevent one party from making an application to the CSA.*

Index

'absent' parents 66
abuse *see* child abuse; violence
acceptability 1
access 41
    inequality 42
    see also contact
Acknowledgment of Service 101
adultery 18, 105
    co-respondents 17
    inequality 2
affidavits 102-3, 105
age 32
allegations, false, of sexual abuse
    72-5
appeals
    interim appeals 25
    to residence orders 58-9, 62
assets 23, 28
    records of 37-8
    see also property
attachment of earnings orders 35
attendance 104

battery
    concealment of 80
    perpetrators 80-1
behaviour, unreasonable 18, 33
budgeting 39
business, records of 38

care of children, weight of rights
    47-8
'caring' parents 66
censure 1, 2
child abduction 87
    breadth of enquiries 88
    complexities 95

consuls on 92-3
contingency records 93-4
conventions in 89-91
as criminal offence 94-5
emergency measures 88-9, 93
increases 89
individuality of cases 90
non-conventions in 91-2
passports and 89
police on 88-9
rulings on 88
support services 95-6
UK conformity 93
Child Abduction Unit 91
child abuse 41
    abhorrence of 71
    alerting of 77
    emotional abuse 76-7
    enquiry shortfalls 71
    evidence 77-8
    neglect 71
    perpetrators 72
    physical abuse 71
    sexual abuse 72-6
child support maintenance
    eligible parties 68-9
    inequality 66-7
    payments 69
    as reform measure 65-6
        reformed 69-70
    shortfalls 68, 69
child support scheme
    child support maintenance
        65-70
    misdescriptions in 66
    shortfalls 65-6, 69
children 29

changing surnames 52-3
custody of 41, 42, 47-8
evidence on abuse 77-8
imagination, truth and 74-5
as minors 12
parental discord and 45, 53-4,
    60-1
perceptiveness 45, 60-1
residence 31, 42-3, 49, 50-1
    overseas 53, 95
Statements of Arrangements
    for Children 100
trauma in 45, 46, 48, 60-1,
    62-3
    from battery 80-1
    from emotional abuse 76-7
    from false allegations 73,
        74
weight of rights 43-4
    inequality 42
wishes of 43-4, 62-3
Children Act 1989 42, 43, 48
Community Legal Service (was
    Legal Aid) 14, 15
community safety units 81, 82
conciliation 47
consuls, on child abduction 92-3
contact 42, 43 see also access
contested divorces 12, 101-2 see
    also individual terms
contributions 31-2, 36
control of children, weight of
    rights 47-8
co-respondents 17
costs
    courts' fees 98
    solicitors' fees 13, 14, 15
counselling
    conciliation 47
    mediation 4-5, 8, 21-2, 27,
        34-5
    Relate 3-5

religion and 5
solicitors and 5
as sounding board 3
timing and 3, 4
courts 103-4, 106
    on child abduction 88
    on childcare 47, 48, 49-50
    directions for trial 102
    on domestic violence 82-5
    equality from 31
    fees 98
    on financial arrangements 28-9,
        30, 34, 35-6
    forgoing 34-5
    individuality of 34
    interim court orders 24-5
    reports to 57-63
custody 41
    inequality 42
    weight of rights 47-8
    see also residence

decrees absolute 106
decrees nisi 104, 106
decrees of judicial separation 7-8
deed of separation 197-200
    equality 9
    legal weight 8-9
defended divorces 12, 101-2 see
    also individual terms
desertion 19, 105
directions for trial 102
distress see trauma
divorce see individual terms
domestic violence 68
    battery 80-1
    emergency measures on 85
    overview of recourse 85
    police on 81, 82-3
    rulings on 83, 84-5
    trials on 82-3
domestic violence units 81, 82

duration of marriage 32-3

earnings 29, 30
    attachment of earnings orders
        35
emergencies
    child abduction as 88-9, 93
    domestic violence as 85
    oral reports for 58-9
emotional abuse
    perpetrators 76-7
    sexual abuse and 76
emotional distress *see* trauma

family assistance orders 54
family court advisers 57
families *see individual terms*
fathers
    named 68
    natural 67, 68
    weight of rights, mothers and
        54-6, 58-9
fees
    courts' 98
    solicitors', minimising 13, 14,
        15
financial arrangements 34
    complexities 27
    equality 27-9
    lump sum orders 35-6
    maintenance 13, 24-5, 27-8,
        30, 35, 65-70
    transfers of property 36
    weight of agreements 24
five-year separations 19, 105
Form E 103
    complexities 39
    on pensions 40

grounds 7
    adultery 2, 17-18, 105
    desertion 19, 105

five-year separations 19, 105
    minimum criteria 17
two-year separations 19, 105
unreasonable behaviour 18, 33,
    105
guilt, complexities 2-3

homes 28, 31
    broken *see individual terms*
husbands *see* spouses

imagination, truth and, children
    74-5
income 29
individuality of cases 31, 33, 34
    in child abductions 90
inheritances 30
interim appeals 25
interim court orders 24-5
irretrievable breakdown 3, 7, 17-19

judges 34, 104
judicial separation, decrees of 7-8

kidnapping *see* child abduction

Land Registry 23-4
Legal Aid (became Community
    Legal Service) 14, 15
Legal Aid Board (became Legal
    Services Commission) 15
Legal Services Commission (was
    Legal Aid Board) 15
length of marriage 32-3
liabilities, records of 38-9
locks, changing 24
lump sum orders 35-6

maintenance 13, 27-8, 30
    child support maintenance
        65-70
    orders 35

reasonable 25
maintenance pending suit 24
marriage
    breakdown *see individual terms*
    conventional 1, 2
    remarriage 1, 2
marriage certificates 97
Marriage Guidance Council
    (became Relate) 3-5
mediation 4-5, 8, 27, 34-5
    as sounding board 21
    weight of agreements 21-2
minor children 12
mothers, weight of rights, fathers
    and 54-6, 58-9

named fathers, inequality in
    maintenance 68
names, children's, changing 52-3
natural fathers
    challenges from 68
    inequality in maintenance 67
neglect, of children 71
no-fault divorce 19
non-molestation orders, on
    domestic violence 83

occupation orders, on domestic
    violence 84-5
oral reports, as emergency measure
    58-9
overseas abductions 87-93
overseas residence 53, 95
overviews ix
    divorce procedure 97-106
    from domestic violence 85
    post-divorce procedure 106-7

parents
    child abuse and, false
        allegations 72-4
    child support maintenance 65-7

concealment by 45
on custody 41, 47-8
discord, children and 45, 53-4,
    60-1
earning capacity 29
emotional abuse from 76-7
fathers 54-6, 58-9, 67, 68
misdescribed 66
mothers 54-6, 58-9
openness from 46
residence 31
trauma in 45, 46, 48, 60-1,
    62-3
weight of responsibilities 43, 48,
    49, 50, 52-3, 65
    inequality 67-8
weight of rights 41
    inequality 42
passports, child abduction and 89
pensions 36, 40
petitioners 11, 97-100, 101-5
petitions 11, 97-100
    cancellation 104-5
physical abuse 80-1
    of children 71
police
    on child abduction 88-9
    on domestic violence 81, 82-3
property 12, 23-4, 28, 31
    transfers of 36
    see also assets
public funding 14, 15

rape 81
reconciliation, late 104-5
records
    as contingency for child
        abduction 93-4
    financial 36-9
reflection 3
refuges 85
registration of land 23-4

Relate (was Marriage Guidance
    Council) 3-5
religion 2
    counselling and 5
remarriage 1, 2
reporters 57, 59, 61-2
    questions to 63
reports to court
    children's wishes in 62-3
    oral 58-9
    preparation 61-2
    recommendations 57, 62
    written 57-8, 60
residence 31, 42-3, 49, 50-1 see
    also custody
residence orders
    appeals 58-9, 62
    conditions 53
    eligible parties 51
    overseas residence and 53
    parents and 54-6, 58-9
    prohibited steps orders 50
    sole and split residence 49
    status quo and 60-1
resources
    assets and property 12, 23-4,
        28-9, 31, 36
    earning capacity 29, 30
    inheritances 30
respondents 11, 100-2, 103, 104-5
    co-respondents 17
restrictions 23-4
Reunite 95

safe houses 85
separation see individual terms
serving 100
sexual abuse
    of children
        false allegations 72-5
        imagination, truth and
            74-5

    increases 72
    perpetrators 72
emotional abuse and 76
investigations 73
investigators, inequality 73, 74
rape 81
social workers 54
solicitors
    confirming need for 12-13
    counselling and 5
    fees, minimising 13, 14, 15
    forgoing 13-14
    hiring 14
    questions to 14-15
Special Procedure List 103-4
spouses 27
    inequality 81
    weight of rights, inequality 2
    see also individual terms
Statements of Arrangements for
    Children 100
status quo, residence orders and
    60-1
stress see trauma
surnames, children's, changing 52-3

tenancies 27
time limits, in adultery 18
timing, counselling and 3, 4
training 30
transfers of property 36
trauma 3, 21, 34-5
    in families 45, 46, 60-1, 62-3
        from battery 80-1
        from emotional abuse 76-7
        from false allegations 73,
            74
trial separations 8
trials, on domestic violence 82-3
truth, imagination and, children
    74-5
two-year separations 19, 105

uncontested/undefended divorces
11, 12, 102
    Special Procedure List 103-4
    see also individual terms
undertakings, on domestic violence
83
unreasonable behaviour 18, 33, 105

video links 77-8
violence 71, 79, 80-1
    domestic *see* domestic violence

wives *see* spouses
Women's Aid 85
written reports 57-8
    delays from 60

MORE BOOKS AVAILABLE FROM **LAWPACK**

Employment Law

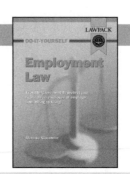

This bestselling guide, by specialist solicitor Melanie Slocombe, is a comprehensive source of up-to-date knowledge on hiring, wages, employment contracts, family-friendly rights, discrimination, termination and other important issues. It puts at your fingertips the important legal points that all employers and employees should know about.

Code B408 | ISBN 1 904053 30 0 | Paperback | 240 x 167mm | 200pp | £11.99 | 6th edition

Wills, Power of Attorney & Probate

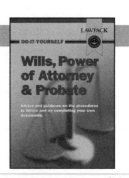

This guide combines three closely related areas of law; the common theme is the management of personal property and legal affairs. In a Will, you set out whom is to inherit your 'estate'; a power of attorney authorises another to act on your behalf with full legal authority; and via probate (or 'Confirmation' in Scotland), executors gain authority to administer your Will.

Code B407 | ISBN 1 904053 33 5 | Paperback | 240 x 167mm | 248pp | £11.99 | 1st edition

Affordable Law

It has been three years since the Government dismantled legal aid; it was anticipated that 'No win, no fee' agreements would – more or less – fill the gap. But this has been met with confusion and misunderstanding, added to which have been the recent consumer scares. This handbook provides guidance on the different means of funding the most common legal actions.

Code B443 | ISBN 1 904053 44 0 | Paperback | A5 | 192pp | £7.99 | 1st edition

To order, visit **www.lawpack.co.uk** or call **020 7394 4040**

MORE BOOKS AVAILABLE FROM **LAWPACK**

Claim Your Cash!

Thousands of people may be eligible for financial help and not know it – this handbook tells them what they could be missing out on. Millions of pounds go unclaimed in welfare benefits each year. This handbook sets out all the main payments you may be entitled to, describing how you go about claiming and giving some useful tips to ensure the best chance of success.

Code B434 | ISBN 1 904053 51 3 | Paperback | A5 | 200pp | £7.99 | 2nd edition

Health & Safety at Work Essentials

Every workplace has to comply with an extensive range of health and safety rules and regulations. With more legal claims being made daily, the price for failing to comply, whether through fines or claims by employees, can be high. This is a handy, 'one-stop' handbook for anyone responsible for health and safety issues in the workplace.

Code B435 | ISBN 1 904053 52 1 | Paperback | A5 | 184pp | £7.99 | 3rd edition

Living Together

How do couples who live together without marrying fare under the law? What are the legal and practical consequences of tying the knot? This handbook provides a thorough analysis of how the law treats married and unmarried couples differently, with respect to children, home ownership, social security, tax and finances, relationship breakdown, Wills and other important issues.

Code B433 | ISBN 1 902646 26 6 | Paperback | A5 | 120pp | £7.99 | 1st edition

To order, visit **www.lawpack.co.uk** or call **020 7394 4040**

MORE BOOKS AVAILABLE FROM **LAWPACK**

Tax Answers at a Glance

We all need to have a hold of the array of taxes now levied by the Government. Compiled by award-winning tax experts and presented in question-and-answer format, this handbook provides a useful and digestible summary of Income Tax, VAT, capital gains, inheritance, pensions, self-employment, partnerships, land and property, trusts and estates, Corporation Tax, stamp duty and more.

Code B425 | ISBN 1 904053 62 9 | Paperback | A5 | 208pp | £7.99 | 4th edition

The Buy-to-Let Bible

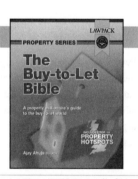

Low mortgage rates and under-performance by traditional savings and investment products means that property has never looked a better way to invest for the future. Author Ajay Ahuja divulges the practical and financial techniques that have made him a millionaire. It covers finding the right property, the right mortgage lender, the right tenant, legal issues and tax.

Code B437 | ISBN 1 904053 36 X | Paperback | 250 x 199mm | 160pp | £11.99 | 2nd edition

Buying Bargains at Property Auctions

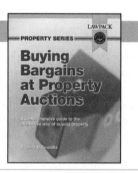

Every week, hundreds of commercial and residential properties are sold at auction in Britain, often at bargain prices, with owner-occupiers accounting for a growing proportion of buyers. In this bestselling guide, author and property auctioneer Howard Gooddie spells out how straightforward the auction route can be and divulges the tips and practices of this relatively unknown world.

Code B426 | ISBN 1 904053 37 8 | Paperback | 250 x 199mm | 176pp | £11.99 | 2nd edition

To order, visit **www.lawpack.co.uk** or call **020 7394 4040**

MORE BOOKS AVAILABLE FROM LAWPACK

House Buying, Selling and Conveyancing

It isn't true that only those who have gone through long, expensive and involved training can possibly understand the intricacies of house buying, selling and conveyancing. This best-selling book explains just how straightforward the whole process really is. Required reading for all house buyers (or sellers).

Code B412 | ISBN 1 904053 61 0 | Paperback | 250 x 199mm | 160pp | £11.99 | 4th edition

Residential Lettings

Are you thinking of letting a flat or a house? This guide steers anyone who intends – or already is – letting property through the legal and practical issues involved. It provides all the up-to-date information and tips that a would-be landlord needs. It will also alert existing landlords to the points of good practice that make a letting successful, and the legal obligations that they may not be aware of.

Code B422 | ISBN 1 904053 63 7 | Paperback | 250 x 199mm | 112pp | £11.99 | 4th edition

Book-Keeping Made Easy

Many businesses fail in their first year or two because of insufficient financial control. This guide provides the new business owner with an understanding of the fundamental principles of book-keeping, showing how to set up accounts and how to benefit from the information they contain.

Code B516 | ISBN 1 904053 06 8 | Paperback | 250 x 199mm | 144pp | £9.99 | 1st edition

To order, visit **www.lawpack.co.uk** or call **020 7394 4040**

MORE BOOKS AVAILABLE FROM **LAWPACK**

Business Letters I Made Easy

Business Letters I and Business Letters II are complementary Made Easy guides, each providing an invaluable source of more than 100 ready-drafted, annotated letters to take away the headache and time-wasting of letter writing. Business Letters I covers managing suppliers and customers, debt collection, credit control and international trade.

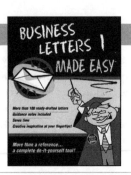

Code B504 | ISBN 1 902646 38 X | Paperback | 250 x 199mm | 160pp | £9.99 | 1ˢᵗ edition

Business Letters II Made Easy

Business Letters II covers employing people, sales and marketing management, banking, insurance and property, business and the community and international trade.

Code B505 | ISBN 1 902646 39 8 | Paperback | 250 x 199mm | 176pp | £9.99 | 1ˢᵗ edition

CVs and Interviews Made Easy

This book provides all-in-one advice on both CVs and interviews under one cover, from putting together a CV that stands out from the crowd, to knowing how to shine at an interview and getting the job you want. It is packed with advice, tips, worksheets, example CVs and real-life case studies from employers and recruitment specialists.

Code B514 | ISBN 1 902646 81 9 | Paperback | 250 x 199mm | 200pp | £9.99 | 1ˢᵗ edition

To order, visit **www.lawpack.co.uk** or call **020 7394 4040**

MORE BOOKS AVAILABLE FROM LAWPACK

Effective PR Made Easy

Raise your profile with some effective PR! Nearly all businesses and organisations benefit from generating public relations activity, be it with customers or other target audiences. The author, Ian Proud, is a seasoned PR professional who tells you from the inside how to get the most out of a PR agency and also how to go about creating effective PR yourself.

Code B518 | ISBN 1 902646 96 7 | Paperback | 250 x 199mm | 132pp | £9.99 | 1ˢᵗ edition

Limited Company Formation Made Easy

Incorporation as a limited liability company is the preferred structure for thousands of successful businesses. This guide explains why, and shows you how to set up your own limited liability company easily and inexpensively. It provides detailed but easy to follow instructions, background information, completed examples of Companies House forms and drafts of other necessary documents.

Code B503 | ISBN 1 902646 43 6 | Paperback | 250 x 199mm | 128pp | £9.99 | 1ˢᵗ edition

Running Your Own Business Made Easy

You have a business idea that you want to put into action, but you also want advice on the realities of setting up and running a business: this Made Easy guide is for you. It takes you through the business-creation process, from assessing your aptitude and ideas, to funding and business plans.

Code B511 | ISBN 1 904053 26 2 | Paperback | 250 x 199mm | 152pp | £9.99 | 2ⁿᵈ edition

To order, visit **www.lawpack.co.uk** or call **020 7394 4040**